TRAINS
TO THE
TRENCHES

TRAINS
TO THE
TRENCHES

THE MEN, LOCOMOTIVES AND TRACKS
THAT TOOK THE ARMIES TO WAR 1914–18

First published in Great Britain
2014 by Aurum Press Ltd
74–77 White Lion Street
Islington
London N1 9PF
www.aurumpress.co.uk

A catalogue record for this book is available
from the British Library.

ISBN 978 1 78131 366 4

10 9 8 7 6 5 4 3 2 1
2018 2017 2016 2015 2014

Design by Joanna MacGregor
Printed in China

This book is dedicated to the men and women who worked on the railways of all combatants on the home fronts as well as the battlefronts. They worked in increasingly difficult conditions as the war went on and their efforts have too often been overlooked. Whatever their nation's cause they served with dedication, distinction and pride.

We remember them.

Above: The German theologian Caspar René Gregory (who was born in America) was reputedly the oldest volunteer in the German army, aged sixty-eight when he was photographed in 1914 next to a carriage on its way to the front.

CONTENTS

INTRODUCTION

The winter of 1916/17 was hard. There were food shortages across Europe after poor weather resulted in a shortage of potatoes, forcing farmers in Germany in particular to plant turnips instead, inevitably leading it to be known as the 'Turnip Winter'. 1916 had seen a war everyone expected to be over quickly in 1914 drag on into its third year and Germany's offensive at Verdun, a British and French attack on the Somme and Russia's Brusilov campaign in Galicia had all proved unsuccessful, at huge cost in men and *matériel* to the nations involved.

Grand assaults on the enemy were impossible in harsh winter weather but the soldiers and horses needed feeding, ammunition and materials supplying, the wounded evacuating and new recruits sent to the battle area. Across huge swathes of France, Belgium, present-day Poland, Hungary, the Czech Republic, Slovakia and even the Middle East railwaymen worked hard to keep their nations' armies furnished with the essentials for survival, let alone warfare.

One of those enginemen was Robert Walker, a Scotsman from Dumbarton, and he found himself and his fireman in an excruciating predicament as far removed from the shellfire, mud and blood of the trenches as it was possible to imagine in France that winter.

It was during the bitter winter of 1916/17. There was considerable activity on the Western Front at that time. We were engaged in transporting troops and munitions from Saulty to the front at St Quentin, trains were loaded up and run through to Longueau outside the city of Amiens. Everything was working like clockwork and we were congratulating ourselves in accomplishing our part in the operations without mishap.

Walker and his fireman, Jimmy Hoon, who had trained at the Great Western Railway's Banbury shed, were working an old goods engine, no. W2728, built by the Midland Railway in the nineteenth century and long past its prime before it was sent to France to supplement Britain's growing contribution to the

Western Front. Their job was to couple to the rear of a heavy train and provide a push from the rear, particularly up gradients. They were, in railway parlance, a banking engine.

We had practically completed the evacuation under almost arctic conditions. The sky was overcast and a bitter East wind had been blowing for three days, making it extremely difficult to prevent our injectors [devices which transfer water from tanks or tenders in steam locomotives into the boiler] from being frozen up. About midday the storm burst in all its intensity and soon the snow covered the rails about a foot high. We pulled out with our last load of army transport wagons and horses about 4.00 pm and as it was our final effort we were determined to get through at all costs and as soon as possible.

No effort was spared in ascending Doullens Bank and despite the retarding effect of the snow which was still driving in blinding sheets we made remarkably good progress. Passing through Candas we made the most of the descent to Canaples and were well on our way up the bank to Flesselles before we lost our momentum. Then it became a battle with the elements and the piled up masses of snow lying in drifts to the depth of three feet in places. Both engines were all out and going hell for leather in a final effort to top the ridge. Passing through Flesselles station we were just beginning to recover after our exertions and picking up speed. I could see a lamp being waved frantically and heard a shout: 'Vitesse, vitesse, le neige est très fond' – 'Faster, faster – the snow is very deep.'

Grasping the import of the message I immediately put the lever full out and pulled the throttle wide open sending the train hurtling through the cutting, which was choked full of snow growing deeper and wreathing up in front as we sought to barge our way through.

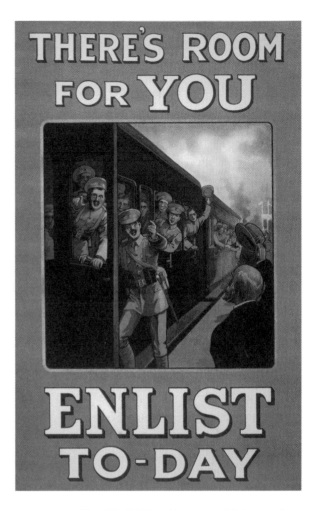

Above: This British recruiting poster used the imagery of troops travelling by train to the front lines to encourage others to enlist.

Walker was taking a calculated risk. Completely unable to see the line ahead he gambled that with enough momentum the train would barge through the snowdrift. If he was wrong and the snow was too deep and tightly packed it would be like hitting a wall. The driver of the leading engine – who probably wouldn't have had a much better view at that time of day and in the conditions – certainly feared so and balked at the task.

Unfortunately the driver of the front engine had shut off steam for some reason unknown with the result we became wedged in, unable to move either back or forward. With the wind shrieking at hurricane force and piling up the snow until we were buried to the level of the cutting above the funnel. Climbing up on top of the vans I could see the front engine uncouple and steam away towards Amiens.

The lead driver *could* have kept his regulator open and helped pull the train through: that he could uncouple so readily suggests that he at least was well and truly clear of the drift. Walker and Hoon now had a real problem.

Our position was now hopeless and clad only in our thin dungarees our plight was really desperate. Making my way over the top of the wagons I came on a flat wagon containing a field gun and limber and in the box I found a pair of old wet blankets and two shovels strapped underneath. With these I returned to the engine and found the fireman huddled up in the corner of the cab almost incapable of action with his clothes frozen stiff like boards. Having brought him back to some semblance of life we rigged up the blankets around the side of the cab and obtained a welcome respite from the piercing wind and cleared the snow from the footboards.

But respite was one thing: while there was fire in the firebox – and Walker and Hoon's lives depended on this now – they could keep themselves from freezing, but if their engine ran out of water they would have to remove the fire from the engine. With no sign of rescue, both men would quickly have suc-

Right: *These American 'doughboys' have arrived on a train formed of French wagons capable of carrying forty men or eight horses. American troops arrived in France from mid-1917.*

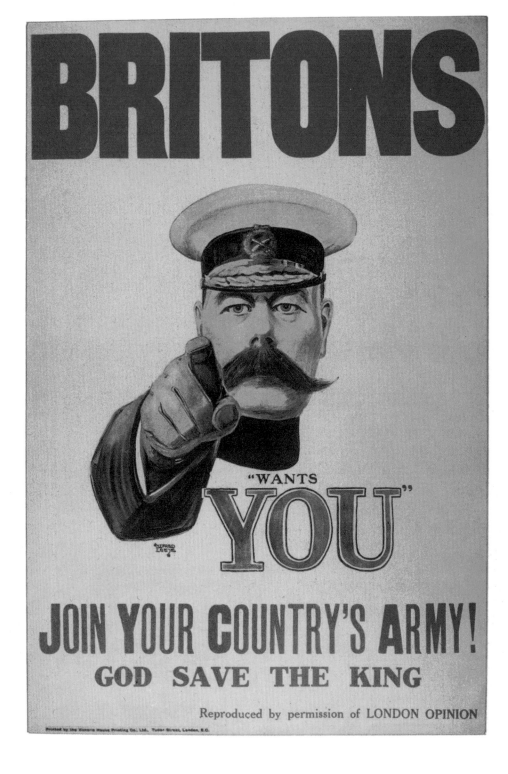

cumbed to hypothermia. Walker examined the tender and found it was just three inches deep. Equally as bad, there was only around eight hundredweight of coal in the tender to feed the fire. Walker made his decision:

Determined to keep my engine efficient and to keep us both from being frozen – already I could feel the frostbite in the tips of my fingers – we got busy with the shovels and filled the tender tank up with great blocks of snow, packing it well down and belting it down with the steam blowing through from the injector. All through the night we laboured on and completed our task at daybreak. I now had a full tank of water but very little coal.

At about 9.00 am we observed a movement being made for our release. Four big powerful engines had been attached to the front of the train and after several ineffectual attempts to move the train there was a crash and three of the wagons were smashed to pieces. The frozen snow had such a grip that the wheels refused to turn and the bufferbeam had been completely torn out from one of the wagons.

The engines returned to Amiens and abandoned the attempt. Next on the scene came the breakdown gang with over a hundred men and officials. They had almost succeeded in clearing the line of debris when their engine failed with frozen injectors so they had no other alternative but to drift back to Bertangles and exchange engines. They returned again in the afternoon with a full train of French engines and about 500 men with picks and shovels. All through the night they worked in relays.

We had not been idle either: we had cut a way from the tender up the bank to the high road and carried the smashed planks and timber from the front of the train back to the engine, which I pushed into the firebox and still maintained steam. That morning another gang of engineers arrived at the other end of the cutting and were hewing their way through to us so we got busy and commenced to dig out our engine. I had literally to chisel the ice out of the valve gear but we accomplished our part and had our engine free and in every way efficient when the two parties of engineers met after clearing the drift. The French official in charge was astounded and would not believe me when I told him we were ready for the road.

Walker and Hoon had survived an ordeal as bad as anyone else behind the front lines that day and they were worried about being court-martialled for being Absent Without Leave as engine failure (though, strictly speaking, Walker's engine hadn't 'failed') was regarded as disobedience of an army order. No investigation was made, and, not surprisingly, Walker didn't volunteer anything. He and Hoon were lucky to survive.

Their experiences were mirrored on both sides of the front line, whether in France and Belgium or on the Eastern Front. Only in the Middle East could they have reasonably expected not to freeze that winter.

It's almost a statement of the obvious that when we read any kind of history most of us unconsciously place ourselves in the situation of the subject and ask a very simple question: 'How would I deal with this?' It's true of railway history, and it's particularly so of military history, and in this centenary year of 2014 many people will be asking how they would have coped with going over the top of the trenches to launch an attack, or with being on the receiving end of an artillery barrage, or dealing with the mud, blood and hardship of conflict.

It was on a train journey from Berlin back to London and then Cornwall that I started pondering what seemed quite a profound question about the railways: 'How would the combatants of 1914 fare if they had to rely on their present-day railway networks?'

It's easy to forget that while the front lines were a war of bullets and shells, such *matériel* was moved most of the way to the front by rail. The First World War of popular imagination is a war of stalemate in the trenches (a view that isn't entirely accurate and certainly not everywhere the war was fought), but it was also, overwhelmingly, a railway war. Whether it was soldiers going to and from the front lines, or sourcing their food, ammunition, letters and supplies; horses and their fodder – a huge need in this pre-motorised age – or the guns themselves, all of the combatants depended to a greater or lesser degree on their rail networks and the ability to use them effectively. The railways were so important that key moments of the war were decided by them: they may have been mostly in the background but they were vital.

And that prompted a related question: 'What was it like for the men and women who manned the trains, who travelled on them and who depended on them so utterly?' What, in fact, was the story of the railways in the First World War? There are good national accounts of aspects of the railway war, but few if any in the English language that pull the strands together. Having written three books on British railway history, I felt it important to look at the wider picture and try to see the situation from the point of view of the other combatants.

The story I discovered is one of brilliant planning, courageous and dedicated men and women, and of limitations that shaped the course of the conflict. And it's a story that starts in Berlin, not far from the incredible present-day *Hauptbahnhof* – main station – where the idea first occurred to me.

Left: *All over Europe and in America soldiers faced lengthy journeys from home to their recruitment centres and then on to training camps and active service. The goodbyes were heartfelt, poignant and all too often final.*

TIMELINE

1914

28 June:
Archduke Franz Ferdinand, heir to Austria-Hungary's throne, is assassinated in Sarajevo.

28 July:
Austria-Hungary declares war on Serbia.

29 July:
Britain calls for international mediation.

31 July:
Russian mobilisation.

31 July:
Railway Executive Committee members provisionally contacted by the War Office.

1 Aug:
Germany declares war on Russia and France mobilises.

3 Aug:
Germany declares war on France.

4 Aug:
Britain declares war on Germany and issues mobilisation order after Germany invades Belgium.

4 Aug:
21,514 route miles of British railways placed under the direction of the Railway Executive Committee.

6 Aug:
Austria-Hungary declares war on Russia and Serbia declares war on Germany.

7 Aug:
French Plan XVII commenced with a series of engagements known as 'The Battle of the Frontiers' and advance parties of the BEF land in France.

8 Aug:
Britain invokes the Defence of the Realm Act (DORA).

10 Aug:
First BEF train arrives at Southampton Docks.

11 Aug:
'Your King and Country Need You' slogan is published in Britain calling for 100,000 men.

12 Aug:
First battalion of the BEF (1st Middlesex) lands at Le Havre, France.

13 Aug:
RFC arrives in France – a Be2 lands at Amiens.

15 Aug:
Serbians win the first Allied victory against the Central Powers at Cer, north-western Serbia.

16 Aug:
Fortress city of Liège falls to German troops.

17 Aug:
Russian 1st and 2nd Armies invade East Prussia.

18 Aug:
BEF Mobilisation largely completed having required 1,408 trains.

19 Aug:
President Woodrow Wilson announces US neutrality.

20 Aug:
Brussels falls to German troops.

21 Aug:
BEF concentration in Belgium and France completed.

22 Aug:
French army defeat near Charleroi signals the end of 'The Battle of the Frontiers' and a general retreat.

23 Aug:
BEF engages German troops at Mons.

24 Aug:
BEF withdrawal from Mons.

25 Aug:
BEF checks German advance at Le Cateau.

26 Aug:
The five-day Battle of Tannenberg begins in East Prussia ending in a Russian defeat.

27 Aug:
First 'Jellicoe Special' of Welsh steam coal departs from Pontypool Road to Grangemouth.

31 Aug:
Amiens captured by German forces.

5 Sept:
First Battle of the Marne begins ending in defeat of the German army.

5 Sept:
HMS *Pathfinder*, light cruiser, the first ship in naval history to be sunk by torpedo.

7 Sept:
First reported use of converted French goods vans as BEF ambulance trains.

9 Sept:
German army retreats northwards to the River Aisne.

11 Sept:
British government issues orders for the raising of a second New Army of six divisions.

15 Sept:
First trench lines are established along the River Aisne.

16 Sept:
Terms of Compensation for British railway companies announced by Board of Trade.

17 Sept:
7 BEF ambulance trains in use in France.

20 Sept:
Royal Engineers acquire first train and help to repair railway lines and bridges near Amiens.

21 Sept:
German New Guinea and surrounding colonies capitulate to Australian Expeditionary Force.

22 Sept:
First British air raid against Germany when Zeppelin bases at Cologne and Düsseldorf are bombed.

26 Sept:
First Indian Army units arrive in France.

28 Sept:
Opening engagements between Russia and the Central Powers on Carpathian, Galician and Polish fronts.

5 Oct:
Three Belgian armoured trains with 4.7-inch guns used against German forces at Antwerp.

9 Oct:
Antwerp falls to German troops.

Oct 13:
Ypres recaptured by British forces.

15 Oct:
Ostend and Zeebrugge occupied by German forces.

16 Oct:
A British Indian Expeditionary Force sails from Bombay to defend Mesopotamia.

19 Oct:
First Battle of Ypres begins.

29 Oct:
Turkey enters the war on the side of the Central Powers.

3 Nov:
Britain declares the North Sea as a military area, effectively creating a blockade of goods into Germany.

5 Nov:
Britain and France declare war on Turkey.

11 Nov:
First Battle of Ypres ends with the defeat of the last German attack.

12 Nov:
First Royal Engineers railway construction and maintenance company arrives in France.

22 Nov:
Continuous trench line established along entire length of the Western Front.

23 Nov:
British troops enter Basra and secure Middle East oil supplies.

8 Dec:
British fleet defeats three German cruisers at the Battle of the Falklands.

16 Dec:
German fleet bombards Hartlepool, Scarborough and Whitby on east coast of England.

21 Dec:
First German aeroplane raid on England.

24 Dec:
Unofficial Christmas truce takes place at various sectors along the Western Front.

1915

1 Jan:
Formation of the Railway Operating Division (ROD).

19 Jan:
First German airship raid on England.

24 Jan:
British naval engagement with German squadrons at Dogger Bank.

31 Jan:
Poison gas used for the first time by the Germans on the Eastern Front west of Warsaw.

1 Feb:
Construction of BEF railway yards and stores depot at Audruicq commences.

2 Feb:
Turkish forces reach the Suez Canal.

7 Feb:
Austro-German

offensives in the Masurian Lakes and Carpathian Mountain regions.

4 Feb:
Germany declares a 'war zone' around Great Britain creating a submarine blockade where even neutral merchant vessels are potential targets.

11 Feb:
1st Division of Canadian Expeditionary Force lands in France.

16 Feb:
French begin a month-long second offensive in the Champagne.

19 Feb:
Allied naval attempt to force the Dardanelles begins.

1 Mar:
Seven SECR 0-6-0Ts hired by ROD to work the military lines at Boulogne.

10 Mar:
First major British Army offensive on the Western Front begins at Neuve Chapelle.

11 Mar:
Britain formally announces blockade of German ports.

22 Mar:
Major Russian offensive in Galicia.

TIMELINE (continued)

1 Apr:
First ROD units formed at Longmoor, Hampshire.

22 Apr:
Second Battle of Ypres begins with the first use of poison gas by German forces on the Western Front.

24 Apr:
First 100 Baldwin 60cm-gauge locos for French use arrive from USA.

25 Apr:
BEF and French army landings at Gallipoli.

1 May:
U-boat sinks the first American merchant ship in the Mediterranean.

2 May:
Start of Austro-German Gorlice–Tarnów Offensive on the Eastern Front.

4 May:
Russians in retreat on Eastern Front.

7 May:
RMS *Lusitania* is sunk by U-20.

9 May:
Failure of British attack on Aubers Ridge prompts 'The Shell Scandal'.

15 May:
British renew offensive action at Festubert.

22 May:
Quintinshill railway disaster near Gretna Green, Scotland.

23 May:
Italy declares war on Austria-Hungary.

25 May:
Herbert Asquith forms British coalition government and Ministry of Munitions created under Lloyd George.

25 May:
Winston Churchill sacked as First Lord of the Admiralty.

May 31:
First Zeppelin raid targets London.

1 June:
BEF REs hire twenty-five Belgian 0-6-0 locomotives.

5 June:
Inaugural conference of British and French ministers to coordinate war policy and strategy held at Calais.

7 June:
Sub-Lt Warneford, RNAS, shoots down German airship LZ37.

12 June:
Further Austro-German advances on the Eastern Front.

29 June:
Italy commences the first of many battles against the Austrians along the Isonzo River.

9 July:
German South West Africa capitulates to General Botha.

13 July:
Combined Austro-German offensive on Eastern Front begins, signalling Russian retreat.

1 Aug:
First Canadian Railway Operating Company arrives in France.

1 Aug:
German air force achieves air supremacy over the Western Front.

Aug 5:
German forces capture Warsaw.

6 Aug:
British landings at Suvla Bay, Gallipoli.

25 Aug:
First Canadian Overseas Railway Construction Company arrives in France.

Sept:
Fifty metre-gauge tram engines ordered from Robert Stephenson and Hawthorn Leslie.

5 Sept:
Tsar Nicholas II takes personal control over Russia's armies.

6 Sept:
Bulgaria enters the war on the side of the Central Powers.

22 Sept:
Major French offensive in the Champagne begins.

25 Sept:
Anglo-French offensive in Artois commences, the British attack at Loos.

28 Sept:
Battle of Kut, Mesopotamia.

30 Sept:
Lord Derby assumes control of recruiting in Great Britain.

Oct:
Russian army is driven out of Poland and Galicia.

5 Oct:
British and French forces land at Salonika.

6 Oct:
Austro-German invasion of Serbia begins.

9 Oct:
Belgrade occupied by Austrian forces.

11 Oct:
Bulgaria invades Serbia.

12 Oct:
Nurse Edith Cavell shot in Brussels by order of a German court-martial.

1 Nov:
ROD operates its first section of stand-

ard-gauge line from Hazebrouck to Pop-erhinge and Ypres.

30 Nov:
Serbian retreat through Albania commences.

Dec:
Fourteen mobile railway cranes now in use with RE, in-cluding thirty-six-ton five-axle Cowans.

7 Dec:
Siege of Kut begins.

19 Dec:
General Sir Douglas Haig replaces Sir John French as Com-mander-in-Chief of the BEF.

1916

8 Jan:
British evacuation of the Gallipoli Penin-sula completed.

27 Jan:
Military Service Act introduces conscrip-tion with effect from 2 March 1916.

8 Feb:
German colony of Cameroon falls to the French and British following seventeen months of fighting.

21 Feb:
German offensive at Verdun begins.

25 Feb:
Fort Douaumont captured by German forces at Verdun.

6 Mar:
German army renews Verdun offensive.

18 Mar:
Russian offensive launched near Vilna and Lake Naroch in response to French request.

Apr:
Three ROD work-shops in operation: Audruicq, Borre and Saint Etienne-du-Rouvray.

1 Apr:
New seventeen-mile standard-gauge line from Candas to Acheux on the Somme sector built by REs and operated by ROD.

10 Apr:
First Manning Wardle petrol tractors arrive in France.

24 Apr:
Outbreak of 'Easter Rising' in Ireland.

29 Apr:
British forces at Kut surrender.

May:
ROD requested to supply all wagon re-quirements (22,500) from their own sources; ROD hires a further 200 Belgian locomotives.

9 May:
British and French governments conclude a working agreement for the eventual partition of Asia Minor.

19 May:
Canadian tramway companies formed to construct 2ft-gauge light railways in Ypres sector.

21 May:
British Summer Time Act implement-ed.

25 May:
British advance from Northern Rhode-sia and Nyasaland across the frontier into German East Africa.

31 May:
British Grand Fleet and the German High Seas Fleet meet in the two-day Battle of Jutland.

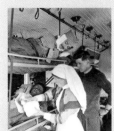

June:
First twenty-eight Baldwin 0-4-0ST for ROD use arrive in France for assembly.

2 June:
Fort Vaux at Verdun captured by German forces.

4 June:
Russian Brusilov Offensive begins on the Eastern Front.

5 June:
Earl Kitchener dies during the sinking of HMS *Hampshire* by a mine off the Scottish coast.

5 June:
Arab revolt against Turkish rule opens with an attack on Medina.

6 June:
Lloyd George ap-pointed Secretary of State for War.

22 June:
German army re-sumes its offensive near Verdun.

23 June:
Fort Thiaumont stormed by German

forces marking the limit of the German advance on Verdun.

24 June:
Start of the week-long Somme bom-bardment in which 1,732,873 shells are fired.

1 July:
Opening battles of the Somme begin.

15 July:
First use of rail-mounted artil-lery by BEF RGA on Somme sector.

20 July:
Railway yards and ammunition dumps at Audruicq heavily bombed by 4 air-ships.

23 July:
Australian forces capture Pozières on the Somme.

25 July:
Reconstituted Serbi-an army comes into action on Salonika front.

24 Aug:
Eric Geddes reports on BEF transporta-tion arrangements in France.

Continued...

TIMELINE (continued)

27 Aug:
Romania declares war on the Central Powers and begins an invasion of Austria-Hungary.

8 Sept:
Rail delivery of forty-nine tanks to the Somme sector.

15 Sept:
Somme battle of Flers-Courcelette and the first use of tanks by the British.

20 Sept:
Russian Brusilov Offensive ends after German reinforcements are moved against it from the Western Front.

24 Sept:
Eric Geddes appointed Director General of Military Railways in France.

Oct:
Order placed for 100 60cm WDLR 'Alco' 2-6-2T engines.

24 Oct:
Fort Douaumont recaptured by French forces.

25 Oct:
First battalion of Canadian railway troops arrives in France.

16 Nov:
First of seventy L&NWR 0-6-0 'Coal Engines' for ROD use arrive in France.

18 Nov:
Concluding battles of the Somme at Beaumont-Hamel.

21 Nov:
Emperor Franz Joseph dies.

6 Dec:
Bucharest captured by German troops.

7 Dec:
Lloyd George becomes Prime Minister of the Coalition Government.

15 Dec:
French attacks at Verdun remove last German threat to the town.

16 Dec:
French C-in-C Joffre replaced by Nivelle.

31 Dec:
Twenty-two railway companies of the REs serving in France.

1917

Jan:
First use of 20hp 60cm-gauge Simplex Petrol Tractors. Numbers would eventually total over 900.

1 Jan:
Women's Land Army set up by British Board of Agriculture.

16 Jan:
British intercept and decode the Zimmerman telegram.

Feb:
ROD acquires partially completed French railway workshops at Saint Etienne-de-Rouvray.

Feb:
New ROD workshops opened at Borre, near Hazebrouck.

1 Feb:
ROD adopts the GCR Class 8K 2-8-0 as its standard engine.

15 Feb:
First L&NWR naval servicemen's special train run from Euston to Thurso, Scotland.

25 Feb:
Reinforced British troops retake Kut in Mesopotamia.

Mar:
First of twenty-six L&NWR G Class 0-8-0s arrive in France.

1 Mar:
Eric Geddes appointed Inspector General of Communications in all BEF war theatres.

11 Mar:
British forces enter Baghdad.

12 Mar:
Russian Tsar Nicholas II abdicates.

15 Mar:
German army begins strategic withdrawal to the Hindenburg Line.

24 Mar:
British commence offensive into Palestine.

31 Mar:
Six Canadian railway battalions now equipped and operating in France.

Apr:
First of sixty-two GWR 'Dean Goods' 0-6-0 locos arrive in France.

4 Apr:
Haig consults Geddes on the timing for the Arras attack.

5 Apr:
German forces complete withdrawal to the Hindenburg Line.

6 Apr:
USA declares war on Germany.

9 Apr:
British forces begin the Battle of Arras.

12 Apr:
Canadian troops capture Vimy Ridge.

16 Apr:
Lenin arrives in Petrograd from Switzerland after crossing Germany in the 'Sealed Train'.

25 Apr:
French offensives on the Aisne and the Chemin des Dames continue.

May:
First Australian Light Railway Operating Company arrives in France.

3 May:
French army units mutiny.

9 May:
French offensive called off.

15 May:
French C-in-C Nivelle sacked and replaced by Pétain.

19 May:
Pershing appointed C-in-C of American Expeditionary Force.

20 May:
Provisional government of Russia announces it will stay in the war and plan a new offensive.

24 May:
Convoy system introduced.

26 May:
Six-day bombardments of Messines and Wytschaete ridges begin with a total of 3,500,000 shells being fired.

27 May:
More widespread French army mutinies.

31 May:
Final delivery of fifty low-level bolster tank carrying bogie wagons from GWR, Swindon.

7 June:
British 2nd Army captures Messines Ridge.

13 June:
London is bombed, suffering its highest civilian casualty rate of the war.

25 June:
Arrival of first American troops in France.

July:
First of fifty NER Class T1 0-8-0s arrive in France.

1 July:
Russian Kerensky offensive begins in Galicia.

6 July:
Aqaba captured by Arab forces.

17 July:
King George V changes royal family name from Saxe-Coburg to Windsor.

19 July:
Austro-German counter-offensive in Galicia results in collapse of Russian forces.

31 July:
Third Battle of Ypres begins.

Aug:
First of seventy-two MR double-framed 0-6-0s arrive in France.

1 Aug:
Eleven GWR 43XX 2-6-0s delivered direct from Swindon to the ROD in France.

4 Aug:
Three thousand Russian troops land in Britain for service on the Western Front.

Sept:
First shipments of GCR Class 8K 2-8-0s arrive in France.

1 Sept:
Germans attack Russian Army at Riga forcing its retreat.

9 Sept:
Mutiny of British troops at Etaples base camp.

20 Sept:
Renewed British attacks at Ypres.

19 Oct:
Colonel T.E. Lawrence destroys the first of many Turkish supply trains on the Hejaz Railway.

24 Oct:
Major Austro-German offensive against the Italians achieves a breakthrough at Caporetto.

1 Nov:
Third Battle of Gaza begins, resulting in defeat of Turkish forces.

6 Nov:
First of five British divisions leave for Italy.

6 Nov:
Canadian troops capture Passchendaele.

7 Nov:
The Bolsheviks successfully overthrow the Kerensky government during the 1917 Russian Revolution.

16 Nov:
Jaffa captured by British forces.

20 Nov:
First large-scale British attack by 381 tanks near Cambrai.

9 Dec:
Jerusalem surrenders to British forces.

9 Dec:
Romania signs armistice with Central Powers.

15 Dec:
Ceasefire agreed between Central Powers and Russia.

17 Dec:
Armistice agreed between the new Russian Soviet government and the Central Powers.

1918

8 Jan:
US President Woodrow Wilson issues his Fourteen Points to peace.

1 Feb:
Rationing introduced in Britain.

6 Feb:
Women enfranchised in Britain for the first time.

10 Feb:
BEF train ferry service introduced from Richborough, Kent, to Calais.

1 Mar:
ROD Light Railway narrow-gauge mileage in France totals 750 miles.

TIMELINE (continued)

3 Mar:
Russia signs the Treaty of Brest-Litovsk, formally ending its participation in the First World War.

9 Mar:
Germany begins to move almost a million men by rail for the Spring Offensive.

21 Mar:
Germany launches Michael Offensive on the Somme sector.

1 Apr:
Formation of the RAF.

5 Apr:
Australian and French troops stand fast at Villers-Bretonneux.

9 Apr:
German Georgette Offensive begins in Flanders.

12 Apr:
Haig issues 'backs to the wall' order.

14 Apr:
Foch appointed C-in-C of Allied forces in France.

21 Apr:
German ace Baron Manfred von Richthofen, 'The Red Baron', is shot down.

24 Apr:
Final German attacks on the Somme are repulsed.

29 Apr:
German attacks in Flanders are halted.

May:
The last Baldwin locomotives are delivered in France, making a total of 415 of all types.

27 May:
German Blucher Offensive begins on the Aisne and the Chemin des Dames.

3 June:
US troops stem German advance at Château Thierry.

9 June:
German attacks in the Montdidier/Noyon region.

15 June:
Abortive Austrian offensive against Italian positions on the River Piave.

26 June:
US troops capture Belleau Wood after twenty days of fighting.

July:
ROD constructs new loco workshops at Rang-du-Fliers, near Etaples.

15 July:
Final German attack in the Champagne/Marne region.

17 July:
Tsar Nicholas and his family murdered by Bolsheviks at Ekaterinberg.

18 July:
Anglo-French counter-offensive on the Marne.

20 July:
German forces retreat from the Marne.

1 Aug:
425 Belgian locomotives at work with American Expeditionary Forces.

8 Aug:
Battle of Amiens and the start of 'The Hundred Days' of Allied progress culminating on 11 November.

Sept:
ROD engines total 1,400 on Western Front allocated to forty-one different depots.

9 Sept:
Amiens to Arras main line reopened for traffic

12 Sept:
US 1st Army captures Saint-Mihiel salient.

19 Sept:
Allies attack Turkish forces at Megiddo forcing a retreat towards Damascus.

26 Sept:
French–US offensive in the Meuse/Argonne region begins.

27 Sept:
British, Australian and US forces break through the Hindenburg Line at Cambrai and Saint-Quentin.

29 Sept:
Bulgaria capitulates and signs armistice.

1 Oct:
Damascus captured.

5 Oct:
Anglo-French forces break through the Hindenburg Line.

10 Oct:
Cambrai captured by Canadian forces.

14 Oct:
German army abandons positions along the Belgian coast and northernmost France.

24 Oct:
Final Italian Vittorio Veneto Offensive opens along the River Piave.

30 Oct:
Turkey signs armistice.

31 Oct:
Hungary withdraws from the union with Austria.

1 Nov:
Belgrade recaptured by Serbian forces.

3 Nov:
Austria signs the Armistice of Villa Giusti effective twenty-four hours later.

8 Nov:
German armistice delegation arrives in the Forest of Compiègne.

9 Nov:
Kaiser Wilhelm II abdicates and flees to Castle Amerongen, in neutral Netherlands.

10 Nov:
German government authorises acceptance of Allied terms.

11 Nov:
Armistice signed in a railway carriage at 5.12 a.m., effective from 11 a.m.

11 Nov:
Emperor Charles I of Austria relinquishes power.

16 Nov:
Allied forces begin march into Germany.

25 Nov:
German forces surrender in East Africa.

1 Dec:
Allied forces cross the German border.

6 Dec:
British troops enter Cologne.

14 Dec:
British General Election sees Lloyd George re-established as Prime Minister.

Dec:
ROD uses 1,660 standard-gauge engines during the conflict, of which 951 were sent from Britain.

1919

Jan:
Staged demobilisation commences for over 3.7 million BEF servicemen.

18 Jan:
Paris Peace Conference opens.

1 Feb:
Introduction of eight-hour working day for British railway staff.

6 Feb:
ROD returns to Belgian and French railways, all lines previously worked by them during the war.

28 Feb:
Traffic on most BEF military lines discontinued.

Mar:
First British ROD engines shipped back to England.

28 June:
Treaty of Versailles signed.

7 Apr:
A total of 2,680,000 wounded conveyed in ambulance trains from British ports since the start of the war.

1 May:
Eric Geddes appointed Minister of Transport.

21 June:
German High Seas Fleet scuttled at Scapa Flow.

15 Aug:
Ministry of Ways and Communications (later the Ministry of Transport) established.

26 Sept:
Second national railway strike over pay.

Oct:
Last British ROD engines shipped back to England except for two retained for leave trains.

5 Oct:
National railway strike action called off.

1920

Jan:
Less than 900,000 servicemen still awaiting demobilisation.

21 Jan:
Inaugural assembly of the League of Nations.

9 Feb:
Eric Geddes presents his cabinet paper 'Future Transport Policy'.

1921

Jan:
Last two British ROD engines retained for leave trains from Cologne returned to England.

15 Aug:
The Railways Act.

1923

1 Jan:
Railways (Grouping) Act of August 1921 implemented.

EMPIRICAL PLATFORMS

EMPIRICAL PLATFORMS

On the back of industrial revolutions and radical new technologies Europe was booming in 1914 – but there were long-standing tensions between the closely related ruling families, and as summer rose they reached boiling point.

In May 1913 the British king George V and Russian tsar Nicholas II joined their cousin Kaiser Wilhelm II of Germany for the lavish wedding of the Kaiser's daughter Princess Victoria Louise to Ernest Augustus, the Duke of Cumberland, in Berlin. The presence of the three heads of state of Europe's most powerful nations wasn't a mere diplomatic exercise: it was a family reunion.

Speaking at the British Embassy on 23 May, the day before the wedding, George V said: 'We are especially pleased that we are the guests of the Sovereign of this great and friendly nation in order to celebrate the union of two young lives which we *earnestly* pray may be fraught with all possible blessing.'

There was a gala performance of *Lohengrin* at Berlin's Royal Opera House; Nicholas drove with Wilhelm to lay a wreath on the sarcophagus of Emperor Wilhelm I at Schloss Charlottenburg – a joyful, happy occasion. But it was the last time the monarchs of Germany, Britain and Russia would meet.

FLEXING THE MUSCLES

German unification in 1871 following Prussia's victory in the Franco-Prussian War unleashed the growing economic potential of the German-speaking states. Industry was powered by coal, and, as with Britain in particular, the products of those industries were moved by railways. All the nineteenth-century industrial revolutions were spurred by the ability of railways to move people, goods and raw materials faster and over greater distances than ever before. Germany boomed.

By 1900 it was threatening Britain's position as the economic powerhouse of Europe. Between 1870 and 1890 Prussia's railway network had quintupled in size, operating a vast, capable and still growing network of routes all the way from Königsberg in the east to Cologne in the west. Much of this expansion was funded directly by the state, helped by Prussia's gradual acquisition of private railways in its territory, which was concluded by 1889.

Opposite, clockwise from top left: Kaiser Wilhelm II of Germany, King George V, Austro-Hungarian Emperor and King Franz Joseph I, Tsar Nicholas II of Russia.

Germany's federal constitution had prevented the creation of a national network but when the *Reichseisenbahnamt* – a national authority created to coordinate Germany's railways – was refocused from mainly looking at Prussia to the whole of the nation the military possibilities came to the fore.

The Minister of War, General von Kaltenborn, proposed a series of strategic rail projects costed at 50 million Marks. Germany's navy – hitherto effectively

Below: Berlin's impressive Lehrter Bahnhof was one of Germany's most important railway stations, and many hundreds of thousands of troops passed through it during the Great War. It is now the site of the incredible Hauptbahnhof – main station – which opened in 2006.

a coastal defence force – was rearming at a rate which alarmed Britain too. In Berlin increasingly the railways became a big political issue. Despite reservations, many of the smaller states joined Prussia to coordinate their railway systems, standardise working practices and rolling stock and coordinate services.

Despite a strong view that France's economic and military potential was waning, Germany's military constantly pressed for rail improvements to ensure it could mobilise troops quickly and efficiently. Routes on the Rhine became a particular focus. If war were to happen the German generals believed that it would be decided in the west. The Schlieffen Plan, completed in 1905 and updated by Helmuth von Moltke, became a cornerstone of German military policy – a cornerstone which depended absolutely on the ability of Germany's rail network to supply the front line with troops and their supplies – and to defeat France within forty-two days giving time to turn eastwards to destroy the slowly mobilising Russia army.

With Belgium the initial target of the Schlieffen Plan, Germany upgraded her rail network with a new railway along the Belgian border from Aix-la-Chapelle to a military camp at Elsenborn, only a few miles from the Belgian frontier. Further connections and railways followed, ostensibly to provide better connections in the region – but from 1908 wayside stations serving hamlets were expanded with 500m-long sidings and locomotive servicing facilities which could handle the trains of an entire army corps. Single-track railways were suddenly expanded to double, and the Germans persuaded the Belgians that better cross-frontier railways would increase trade. They also conveniently served military camps where troops could assemble. The tracks through Troisvierges in Luxembourg were doubled too, an easy thing for the Germans to do given that they controlled the Luxembourg rail network, even though Luxembourg had been an independent and

The famous German Field Marshal von Moltke the Elder said in 1879:

' *Railways have become, in our time, one of the most essential instruments for the conduct of war. The transport of large bodies of troops to a given point is an extremely complicated and comprehensive piece of work, to which continuous attention must be paid. Every fresh railway junction makes a difference, while, although we may not want to make use of every railway line that has been constructed, we may still want to make use of the whole of the rolling stock that is available.* '

neutral state since the Treaty of London in 1839 – later reaffirmed by a second treaty in 1867.

It was no different in the east, where Germany bordered the Russian Empire. As well as the east–west routes linking the principal cities, a series of north–south railways was built paralleling the likely front lines, and with branch lines towards the frontier to allow troops to be concentrated.

For years French spies had ranged across western Germany and reported back on railway construction: five double-track railways across the Rhine and other developments strongly suggested that Germany would ignore Belgian neutrality and attack on the north-eastern frontier. They saw huge spreads of sidings with no possible commercial purpose; extended platforms to cater for passengers who would never arrive, facilities for fuelling and servicing locomotives in areas where it made no operational sense for existing services. They were nothing less than professional train-spotters and their accounts alarmed and informed the powers that were in Paris. Germany's railways were being prepared for war: the unanswerable question was whether they were intended to feed troops into the attack or the defence.

It wasn't just the French who spotted the German preparations either. The American writer Roy Norton wrote in *The Man of Peace*:

Right: *Reserves depart from Görlitzer station in Berlin in late 1914, with a military brass band sending them off.*

On February 14 of this year [1914] I was in Cologne, and blundered, where I had no business, into what I learned was a military-stores yard. Among other curious things were tiny locomotives loaded on flats which could be run off those cars by an ingenious contrivance of metals, or, as we call them in America, rails. Also there were other flats loaded with sections of tracks fastened on cup ties [sleepers that can be laid on the surface of the earth] and sections of miniature bridges on other flats. I saw how it was possible to lay a line of temporary railway, including bridges, almost anywhere in an incredibly short space of time, if one had the men ... Before I could conclude my examination I discovered that I was on verboten ground; but the official who directed me out told me that what I had seen were construction outfits.

They were indeed construction outfits – for military *Feldbahn*. Germany developed this system – which translates literally as 'field railway' – to take supplies from the nearest railhead even closer to the front line.

Based on tracks with a gauge of 600mm (the standard gauge is 1,435mm) and with specially developed steam locomotives and wagons, this small railway could be laid quickly and easily and cross rougher ground than a full-size railway. It was almost like a train set to build, with tracks preassembled into short lengths which could be laid easily and quickly with the minimum of men and equipment.

So, by 1913 Germany had developed strategic rail networks near the borders of France, Luxembourg, Belgium, the Netherlands and Russia, had improved rail links with Austria-Hungary and expanded facilities to handle vast numbers of troops near those borders. But it wasn't just Europe that Germany's rail plans affected.

Its ally, Austria-Hungary, had developed its rail network too, building 16,000 miles of railway from 1880 to 1900 as part of a concerted strategy to link its disparate and fractious empire.

GRAND AMBITIONS

'In spite of the fact that we have no such fleet as we should have, we have conquered for ourselves a place in the sun. It will now be my task to see to it that this place in the sun shall remain our undisputed possession, in order that the sun's rays may fall fruitfully upon our activity and trade in foreign parts, that our industry and agriculture may develop within the state and our sailing sports upon the water, for our future lies upon the water' – Kaiser Wilhelm II from a speech in Hamburg, 1901, quoted by Alexander Duncan McLaren in *Germanism from Within* (1916).

The Kaiser's quote explains many of Germany's ambitions. As a growing economic power it wanted an empire to rival those of other European countries in order to gain access to raw materials, new markets and political power. Germany's domestic rail expansion was only part of a wider picture. In very simple terms it wanted to secure an empire along the lines of the British to extend its influence and railways

quickly became a key tool of this policy.

Fundamental to this was a proposal to build a railway all the way from Berlin to Baghdad, running through the Ottoman Empire.

From the late 1880s Germany had extensive influence in the Ottoman Empire, thanks to the Kaiser's blossoming relationship with Sultan Abdul Hamid II, and from 1909 the Empire's ruler. German interests had funded the Anatolian Railway linking Constantinople with Ankara and Konya. A railway reaching all the way to Baghdad offered scope for a port on the Persian Gulf and eventually connections to Germany's colonial possessions in Africa. The Ottomans saw it as a way of countering Russian influence in the region, and the Germans a way of evading Britain's control of the seas, on whose goodwill the transport of materials and men depended. It would also provide Germany with direct access to huge resources of oil, which was becoming increasingly important for industry and transport. Although the battleships coming off the slipways in the early twentieth century were coal-powered, designs were in hand for a new generation of oil-powered behemoths that were faster, more powerful and with a longer range than their predecessors.

Britain, already alarmed by the massive growth of Germany's High Seas Fleet, viewed the proposal with mistrust. Initial support on the basis of the country's historically close relationship with Germany waned as the importance of oil and the potential loss of its monopoly on important trade routes became clear. Proposals by the Ottomans to increase customs duties to build the railway were blocked by Britain, France and Russia (approval from all was needed for customs increases following the Ottomans' default on loans in 1875) but construction began, albeit tardily. The project wasn't completed by 1913 but it helped cement the already strong relationship between Germany and the Ottomans – and added even more to the rising tension between Germany and its European neighbours.

THE FRENCH CONNECTIONS

It wasn't just Germany that was viewing its railways with a strategic if not explicitly military bent. France had lost the provinces of Alsace and Lorraine after the Franco-Prussian War and after a prolonged spell in the doldrums was beginning to stir.

Its railways operated as private companies but with extensive regulation from the state and grand plans to enhance the country's rail network and spread the benefits of railways to as many of its citizens as possible. Government subsidy made a huge expansion of the rail network possible, with the state expecting a return on its investment from the private companies it supported. It was an awkward hybrid between the nationalised Prussian model and the completely private British model that suffered continuous internal conflict about investment and particularly goods rates.

Tunnels through the Alps linking France with Italy and Switzerland were planned and improved routes to ports such as Le Havre created and a grand dream of a continuous railway between Calais and Marseilles revived. The imperatives may have been commercial and social but better links would also undoubtedly benefit the military too. Drawing on the lessons of the Franco-Prussian War in which the Prussians' use of railways was widely felt to have been decisive, France began to rebuild.

The military had a major influence on its rail expansion, particularly where routes approached the frontier with Germany. There were concerns about whether new routes offered better logistics for the French or an easy way in for the Germans. Even so, platforms were extended at stations, timetables prepared and plans developed to mobilise troops rapidly across France's eastern frontier.

France's economic power meant that it would never be able to match the investment of Germany, but, nonetheless, when Princess Victoria Louise married in 1913, its rail network was comprehensive and well planned. Its core routes centred on Paris, unlike in Germany, where the presence of so many significant regional cities lent itself to a spider's web of railways. And with Paris now rather closer to the German border (some 100km) than it was before the Franco-Prussian War thanks to the loss of Alsace and Lorraine, France would be able to deploy troops and supplies to any war in the east quickly and effectively.

RUSSIAN EXPANSION

As with France and Germany, in the early 1900s Russia too was modernising and expanding its rail network. From just over 14,000 miles of track in 1880, by 1905 its network had reached almost 32,000 miles and was being extended rapidly so that in 1914 it had 45,350 route miles. The need was acute: with vast territories poorly linked by roads, railways offered the only way of moving people and goods – and, of course, troops – rapidly across country.

Russia's rail network differed from those in Germany and much of continental Europe by having a different track gauge. Whereas the major countries of Europe (with the exceptions of Spain and Portugal) adopted the British standard of 1,435mm (4ft 8½ inches) Russia adopted a gauge of 1,524mm, or 5ft. The importance of railways in military applications was recognised very early in Russia and it was felt that adopting a different gauge would make it difficult if not impossible for invaders to run their standard-gauge trains over Russian tracks. The reverse would also apply to Russia, and the only way to resolve this would be to laboriously remove a rail, shift it to the gauge required and fix it in place. In peacetime this is a time-consuming and exacting task. Under fire in wartime it would be massively more difficult.

By 1913 Russia had built main-line railways to its key cities and frontiers and was working towards the German model to ensure troops could be moved east–west and north–south. Russia's problem was that

the area involved was vast and the population thinly spread: funding the comprehensive network needed to ensure total mobility for its troops was always going to be a long-term ambition at best. In 1913 the reality for Russia was that its troops were likely to have to march long distances from their railheads to the front line. And this, the Germans felt, meant that Russia's mobilisation would be a lengthy process.

The great European powers had invested heavily in their armed forces, and all bar Britain had given a lot of thought to how they could use their railways to support armies on the offensive or defensive. Britain, secured by the Royal Navy and only now realising the implications of becoming involved in a continental war for which its professional but small army was

Above: As war was declared civilians relied on newspapers – and often extra editions – to keep them abreast of the news. 'Call to arms' is the headline on the Deutsche Tageszeitung *– German Daily Newspaper – on 1 August 1914, announcing the mobilisation of German forces.*

Next page: Soldiers of all sides chalked hopeful messages of the war's hoped-for outcome on the trains they travelled on to the front lines – this image appears to be genuine, but propagandists sometimes added detail to other pictures after they were taken to amplify the point.

ill-prepared, could at least exercise a degree of choice about whether it got involved and how. Tensions were rising across Europe. The fire had been built and the tinder was dry. All it now needed was a spark to set a continent ablaze.

THE PRESSURES BUILD

The events which led to the start of the First World War have been explained so often it almost seems redundant to do so again, but critical assumptions about the capabilities and limitations of rail networks played a vital part in the actions that followed the assassination of Archduke Franz Ferdinand in Sarajevo on 28 June.

There was widespread anger in Austria-Hungary following the assassination and it provided the justification Austria had long sought to invade Serbia – to rid themselves of a difficult neighbour and to help address internal difficulties, of which there were many, most notably innumerable disaffected minorities which the ruling Hapsburg dynasty did little to ameliorate. Austria-Hungary had civil rights turmoil in the recently annexed Bosnia-Herzegovina (1908), conflicting regional government and judicial policies, and divisive multi-language barriers, among just some of its problems.

Germany unequivocally backed Austria. In Max Hastings' *Catastrophe: Europe Goes to War 1914*, the Austrian envoy to Wilhelm II is reported as quoting the Kaiser: 'If we really saw the necessity for military action against Serbia [I] would think it regrettable if we did not take advantage of the present moment, which is favourable from our point of view.'

The Germans seemed to believe that an invasion of Serbia would be a local conflict without wider ramifications. They knew that Russia would probably seek to protect Serbia, as it had long promised, yet they also believed that Russia's military build-up would soon make any war with it unwinnable. If war was to happen with Russia, Germany believed it

had only a limited window of opportunity in which to win it as Russia was rapidly developing its economy, transportation network and military capacity. By 1916, the Germans believed, a war against Russia could only lead to defeat. For their part, Russia and France believed the Germans were bluffing. Only on 23 July 1914, when Austria presented an ultimatum to the Serbs making demands no nation would willingly accept, did conflict move from a possibility to a probability.

Russia quickly offered conditional support to the Serbs, but the Serbs accepted all of the terms of Austria's ultimatum except for the requirements for Austrians to have *police* authority within Serbia, to apprehend the assassins, carry out legal proceedings and suppress subversive elements.

It mattered little. Serbia knew that Austria was unlikely to accept even this and so it ordered its depleted and under-equipped army to mobilise. Austria followed quickly, inventing an attack on a Danube steamer to justify its own mobilisation.

Russia now moved speedily and began a partial mobilisation, first in the four military districts bordering the Austro-Hungarian border, a process it had begun within an hour of learning of the Austrian ultimatum. Its rail network needed twelve days' notice of this and it would take a month for its armies to deploy fully. Events were now moving at a pace beyond the control of the primitive communications networks available to governments. On 28 July Austrian Emperor Franz Joseph signed the declaration of war.

It was now a race between the great powers – Germany, France and Russia – to mobilise their forces first. If their potential enemy beat them to it, their soldiers would be fighting at a huge disadvantage.

Germany decided to mobilise and issue an ultimatum to Belgium demanding free passage through its territory. Baron de Gaiffier d'Hestroy, the political director of Belgium's Foreign Ministry, was recalled from holiday in Switzerland and found that Germany and Austria-Hungary had already taken over trains to move troops.

Russia officially announced its mobilisation first, on 31 July. A day later Germany declared war on Russia, claiming that the deployment of Russian forces represented 'a grave and imminent danger' for the German Empire.

France was mobilising too, well awake to the danger the Germans posed. Britain had deployed its Grand Fleet to Scapa Flow to enforce a distant blockade of Germany and back in 1839 had promised to defend Belgium's neutrality. Germany was sceptical about whether Britain would become involved in a conflict which apparently threatened few of its interests, but Britain now had to decide how much involvement it would have. Support for Belgium was strong, but there was also a powerful isolationist lobby. Nobody outside the closest circles of government knew whether Britain would go to war on a matter of principle.

And still the troop trains ran from Cologne towards Germany's borders, one every three or four minutes estimated the Belgian vice-consul in the city. The trains were heading for the Belgian border rather than the French, concentrated at Aix-la-Chapelle. Germany used 11,000 trains to mobilise its forces and France 7,000. In total, Germany had 1.9 million regular troops and Austria-Hungary 1.1 million; Russia 1.4 million, France 1.3 million, Belgium 186,000 and Britain 120,000 soldiers available for service abroad.

The forces were massing on western and eastern fronts. Germany issued its ultimatum to Belgium on 2 August demanding free passage for its soldiers. The

RAILWAYS OF THE COMBATANTS, 1914

COUNTRY	ROUTE MILES	NO. OF LOCOMOTIVES	NO. OF CARRIAGES	NO. OF WAGONS
UNITED KINGDOM	23,718	22,998	72,888	780,520*
BELGIUM	5,370	4,300	1,000	90,000
GERMANY	38,950	28,000	60,000	600,000
FRANCE	31,200	14,500	33,500	364,000
RUSSIA	45,350	17,200	20,000	370,000
AUSTRIA-HUNGARY	28,400	10,000	21,000	245,000

* Excludes an estimated 600,000 wagons owned by private companies such as coal mines, steelworks and so on.

Above: Russia's Trans-Siberian railway was approaching full operation at the start of the Great War, and a train pulls into Irkutsk, two-thirds of the way from Moscow to Vladivostok on this 5,800-mile-long route.

world was on the brink – and waiting either for the Kaiser to blink or for someone to fire the first shot.

WAR BY TIMETABLE?

The historian A.J.P. Taylor's famous theory that the detailed plans drawn up by combatants to mobilise their forces quickly by rail as a deterrent started an inexorable process that led to war is repeated so often it is almost regarded as historical fact. But it's a theory which doesn't stand detailed examination.

It is true to say that railways allowed the mobilisation of forces faster and in better condition than ever before, and that all the major powers had developed elaborate plans to achieve this; but to suggest that setting a mobilisation in motion was unstoppable falls foul of the basic rules of railway operation developed in the nineteenth century and still used in their fundamental form today.

Trains are only allowed to travel on a section of track – except in very specific circumstances, such as recovering a failed train – when it has been proved there are no other trains in it. A section might be one mile long, or ten, or even a whole branch line if only one train was due to operate on it, but the principle is that while a train is in a section nothing else is allowed to be on the same stretch of track. This came early in the days of railways after a series of accidents where a given time was allowed after a train had departed before sending the next one along with no way of knowing whether it had broken down around the next corner.

The status of the sections was indicated by signals that were raised or lowered (it depended on the railway as to which) to indicate that the track was occupied. The underlying assumption on all of Europe's railways was that the railway was occupied unless a signal gave explicit permission for a train to proceed. This was controlled by signalboxes along the route which operated the signals; when a train passed them they sent a telegraph signal to the 'box behind that the route was now clear. Only then was the signal changed to allow a train to proceed. Failure to abide by these rules could and did, as we shall see in Chapter 4, lead to accidents.

For Taylor's theory to hold true it has to be accepted that it was impossible for trains to be prevented from reaching their destination – that if the tracks were clear they could not be stopped. In the normal course of events there would be no reason to stop trains if the section(s) ahead was clear – but the telegraph allowed sophisticated communication between signalboxes via bell codes. If an accident blocked the tracks ahead, for example, an emergency code was sent out instructing signalmen to stop all trains regardless of whether or not the route immediately ahead of them was clear. An 'all lines blocked' instruction on the telegraph meant just that and all trains in the vicinity were halted at the next signal.

Although Germany's operating system was different in its execution it would have been simple to halt the trains at main stations such as Cologne and Aachen pending further instructions. Doing this would have caused disruption and dislocation across huge swathes of the railway network, but it was perfectly possible with the technology of the time. In fact, halting the mobilisation of troops on trains was vastly easier than if the armies had travelled on foot: that would have required despatch riders to provide instructions.

Taylor's oft-repeated belief that once mobilisation started it could not be halted, and that war was inevitable, is false: the ability was there, but for the Germans the desire was not.

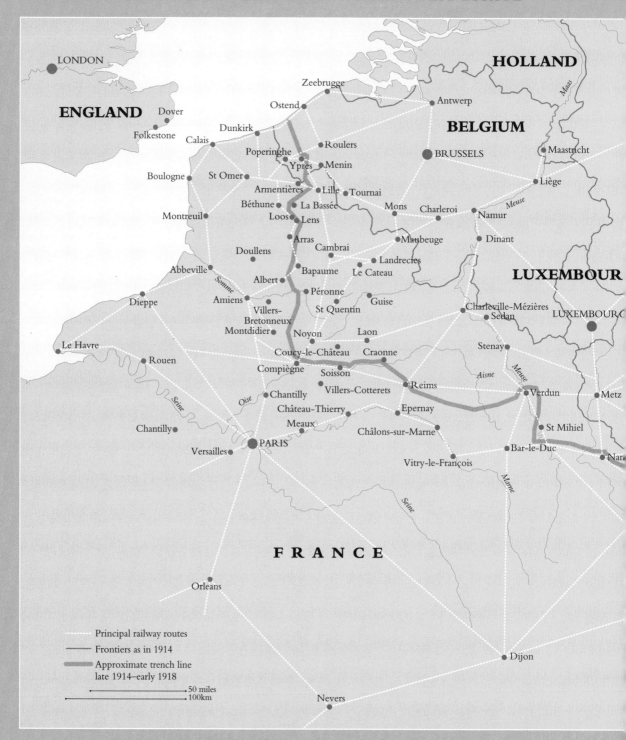

The map shows the trench line approximately as it stabilised to become the Western Front from late 1914 to early 1918. The exact front lines fluctuated throughout the conflict, with many of the locations in north-west France in particular changing hands more than once. The extent of the rail networks is clearly seen in the Thomas Cook railway maps reproduced in the Conclusion.

2

OPENING SHOTS

OPENING SHOTS

Germany planned to beat France before Russia and it intended to use its railway network to switch troops to the Eastern Front after the French surrender. The need was for speed and assumptions about how the opposition would react proved fatal to the generals' ambitions.

By the end of 3 August, Germany's railways had delivered troops, their horses and supplies to railheads on the Belgian frontier in one of the most brilliant railway operations ever undertaken. To move one German army corps – around 2.5 per cent of the total in 1914 – required 170 coaches for officers, 965 for infantry, 2,960 wagons for cavalry and 1,915 for artillery, and about the same number of vehicles to transport all of their supplies. If it had been a peacetime exercise, it would be deservedly lauded even today.

Nowadays it is a long journey from Berlin to the Belgian border on Deutsche Bahn's brilliant electric ICE trains but in 1914 it was much longer. The War Correspondent of the *Daily News*, H.W. Nevinson, reported on leaving Berlin for neutral Holland with the British Ambassador and his staff on 6 August:

> For twenty-four hours the train carried us all slowly lumbering through North Germany to the Dutch frontier. On our way we passed or were impeded by uncounted railway vans decorated with boughs of trees and crammed with reservists going to the Belgian front. The men had now chalked Nach Bruxelles or Nach London as well as Nach Paris on the vans and at every station they were met by bands of Red Cross girls bringing coffee, wine and food. At all the larger stations, too, the news of our train's approach had been signalled, and to cheer us on our way all the old men, boys and women of the place had flocked down with any musical instruments they could collect, and, standing, thick on the platform, they played for us the German national tunes, 'Deutschland, Deutschland' predominating. They played with the persistence of the German bands known to me in childhood. Sometimes, to impress their patriotism more distinctly upon us, they brought their instruments close up to the carriage windows, and the shifting tubes of the trombones came right into the carriage …

At 8 a.m. on 4 August, German troops crossed the border at Gemmerich. The invasion of Belgium had begun. From the beginning Germany's war plans

depended utterly on speed. A quick passage through Belgium to the French border was vital if Paris were to be encircled and France beaten. The need for speed was hastened by Russia's unexpectedly swift mobilisation as Germany's forces were comprehensively outnumbered by those of France and Russia. Any delays would allow the Triple Entente to prepare their defences.

MISGUIDED ASSUMPTIONS

As with every major war plan, once Germany's troops crossed the border into Belgium their success or failure depended on the ability of her own troops, the actions of the enemy, and the underlying assumptions behind the overall strategy. Belgian resistance

was expected to be slight, and, indeed, at the frontier post it was, but to Germany's chagrin Belgium had decided to fight against it. Any hope of a clear run to the French border was dashed, but on the morning of 4 August there was no reason for Germany to believe that it wouldn't achieve its ambitions.

Yet Belgium had used just a handful of days' grace to prepare well. Key railway bridges, tunnels and junctions were prepared for demolition and rolling stock moved away from the frontier and hidden. Her

Above: Photographs of the destruction of railway infrastructure in 1914 are very rare, but whether early or late in the conflict engineers faced huge challenges in rebuilding the tracks and the bridges in battle zones. This is a road overbridge at the north end of Albert station in October 1918.

GERMANY'S MILITARY RAILWAY ORGANISATION

Germany's equivalent of the Railway Operating Division (ROD), the Militär-Eisenbahn-Direktion (Military Railway Directorate), controlled railways in occupied territory. It oversaw manufacturing, rolling stock, workshop and planning functions to support the German armies.

To improve liaison between military railways and the civilian networks in occupied countries that supplied them, another organisation, the Militärgeneraldirektionen der Eisenbahnen (Military General Agencies of the Railways), was formed with offices in Brussels, Warsaw and Bucharest.

By the end of 1915, 144,000 men were employed in the combined military railway operations, of whom 41,000 were soldiers, 54,000 officials from Germany and 49,000 auxiliaries from the occupied areas, often existing railway staff. By 1918 the figures had risen further. In addition to 108,000 soldiers 70,000 German railway staff were sent abroad, and 45,000 prisoners of war also worked on the railways.

THE NORD RAILWAY

The Compagnie Chemin du Fer du Nord – usually referred to as the Nord Railway – bore the brunt of the Allied war effort on the Western Front. Created in 1845 with a remit to build a railway from Paris to Lille and Valenciennes, which opened in 1846 to connect with existing railways from Lille to Belgium, it expanded rapidly and by 1914 operated a comprehensive network of main lines and branches across northern and eastern France and had a subsidiary operation in Belgium called Compagnie du Nord – Belge.

It operated one of the densest and most heavily used rail networks in the world, with a route mileage of around 2,500 encompassing some of France's most important industrial areas.

Taken under government control – as were all French railways – in 1914 it suffered heavily with far higher than normal traffic levels in addition to damage caused by the fighting on the Western Front.

Manpower shortages caused by staff joining the army, the loss of parts of its network to the Germans and low rates of recruitment led to inevitable maintenance issues across its fleet, leading, in turn, from 1916 onwards, to a growing British and Commonwealth involvement in its operation.

The company continued to innovate after the Great War, producing the famous 'Superpacific' express passenger locomotives from 1923 that offered a performance far better than any British equivalent.

THE PRUSSIAN RAILWAYS 'P8'

The Prussian Railways 'P8' 4-6-0 was one of the main workhorses of the war. Handsome and powerful, it hauled passenger and freight trains across Germany and many of its occupied territories throughout the First World War.

The design was a 'simple' – non-compounded – locomotive with two cylinders and easy to maintain outside valve gear and driving wheels of 1,750mm diameter (approximately 5ft 9 inches). This combination made for an ideal general-purpose locomotive that was able to haul heavy loads without slipping and, with a top speed of 68mph, more than adequate for duties of the era. Furthermore, its axle load of 17.36 tons meant that only the most lightly constructed railways were prohibited to it.

Most construction was by Berliner Maschinenbau, which designed the locomotives, but as the war progressed other builders took on the workload, too, and from 1908 when construction began, to 1926 when it ceased, more than 3,700 had been built, although some of these were in other countries.

The 'P8s' had long careers in Germany, the last survivors not being withdrawn until 1974 – long after Britain had dispensed with steam traction – and many operated in other countries as reparations after the Great War.

troops were motivated and determined, and confident they would give the invaders pause when the invasion began.

The first place the Germans met real resistance was at Liège, based at the confluence of the Meuse and Orthe rivers, and a major obstacle on the invasion route to France. With twelve forts mutually supporting each other in a ring, and 30,000 troops of Belgium's 100,000-strong army, Liège was a potential stumbling block for the Germans, and so it proved. It took an eleven-day siege finally to eliminate resistance, and although the Germans needed to concentrate their forces before moving on, it still delayed the advance by some three or four days.

As brave as the Belgian resistance at Liège was, demolition of railway infrastructure probably hurt the Germans more. To keep the troops, horses and artillery supplied Germany needed to get trains running over Belgian rails quickly. In some places it could, but where extensive repairs were needed to bridges, tunnels or key junctions not nearly enough trains could run. The German army would have to march much further than it anticipated, giving France time to prepare its defence. The error of Germany's two assumptions – that Belgium would be a walkover, and that it could supply its armies by rail throughout the advance – slowed the invasion.

France was now fully mobilising. Philippe Masson, member of the *Comité d'histoire de la Deuxième Guerre mondiale* and former lecturer at the Naval War College of France, wrote:

All over the country, down to the smallest village, church bells were rung and the first yellow mobilisation posters were stuck on post office walls. All the reservists of the years between 1887 and 1910 were recalled. Almost 3,000,000 men responded to the 'call to arms' without a murmur. On Sunday, 2 August, ordinary day-to-day life ceased. Mobilisation was carried out promptly, even

enthusiastically. Outside barracks and in front of railway stations thronged crowds of men who had been mobilised, carrying suitcases and parcels, surrounded by women and children, many of whom were weeping. There were shouts and cries as the men clambered into the goods wagons which had inscriptions scrawled on their side: 'To Berlin. We'll get them'. In Paris, at La Gare de l'Est, a convoy got under way every quarter of an hour. 'The first day of mobilisation was gay and splendid like a public holiday,' said Le Figaro. *The General Staff expected at least 13 per cent of those called up to default, but in fact, not even 1.5 per cent did so.*

Britain's plans envisaged the deployment of the British Expeditionary Force (BEF) and mobilisation began at midnight on 4 August. Although Britain wasn't ready for a continental war it had planned how it would send its small force to France. Soldiers and horses alike were sent to entrainment points and the first special train reached Southampton – the key embarkation port for France – at 8.15 on 10 August. In a fortnight 334 special trains took 69,000 troops to Southampton, from where they sailed to the Continent.

Once in France, Britain relied on France's rail network to take them to the front (although at this stage the war was fluid and fixed front lines hadn't been established). This was perfectly sensible: not only did Britain not have an extensive and dedicated railway corps to run its own trains, but the rules of operation on French railways were quite different from those in Britain, and operating its own trains independently would have caused confusion and a major timetabling headache, if not accidents. The key railhead for the British was Amiens, a junction station with good links to the Channel ports, the Belgian border and Paris. It was easy for troops and supplies to get from the ports or from the rest of France, and

to the front line. It would become a vital aspect of British and French military and railway operations almost for the duration of the war.

The French approach to its railways in wartime was brilliant. As France mobilised it placed its railways under the control of the military authorities, allowing operational and strategic needs to take priority over civilian travel and the conflicting demands of private railway companies. Wartime timetables were introduced immediately and railway staff mobilised to operate them. Each *réseau* – company network– was managed by a joint commission of a railway official and an army staff officer created before the war to ensure smooth operation. Each route's capacity was carefully evaluated and a certain number of trains timed to run over it every day. It helped greatly that the formations and speeds of trains were standardised immediately. An infantry battalion, for example, would board one train which would run at 12mph, and this was the standard through France. It is true that some trains could have run faster, and *in extremis* they did, but in adopting a national standard France made planning trains and rolling stock much more straightforward, and in wartime simplicity is a precious and often scarce commodity. The simplicity extended to the transport of men and horses. Officers may have travelled in carriages, but the bulk of the troops travelled in covered wagons that could either carry forty men or eight horses. In almost every account, the 'Hommes 40 Chevaux 8' label on the wagons is described as 'infamous' or 'notorious'

Previous page: *Although the British used Chinese labour, much of the rebuilding was undertaken by skilled engineers, such as these British soldiers in France later in the war.*

Right: *Engineers were forced to improvise, and in order to get trains running quickly resorted to temporary wooden structures such as this over the Celle river at Pont de Metz, near Amiens. Speeds of trains were limited, but even heavy locomotives were able to travel over them. This work was carried out by 8th Railway Company, Royal Engineers.*

or some other pejorative term. In practice, though, it was a pragmatic approach by the French railways. They may not have travelled in Pullman luxury, but soldiers were sheltered, warm and, crucially, not tired out by lengthy marches. Using wagons that could carry men or horses provided greater flexibility than having dedicated vehicles for both.

France's attention to detail extended to provision of supplies. It had been a long-standing practice in civil goods trains for many to pick up and drop off wagons as they went along. In wartime France, as far as military trains were concerned, this practice was

largely abandoned. Instead, bulk trains comprising a single commodity – perhaps fodder for horses, or ammunition, or food or any of the myriad needs of an army – were delivered to a *gare régulatrice* (regulating station) from where these bulk trains were split and reassembled with other supplies to form the mixed trains needed to supply formations at the front. What this offered, again, was flexibility to respond to the changing demands of military units. A train carrying a given mix of ammunition, food and fuel over long distances right to the front might not actually have the right balance of stores when it reached its destination. The *gare régulatrice* system meant that train loads to the front-line units could be varied to meet changing circumstances almost up until the last minute.

France's initial moves were to try and attack Germany through Alsace and Lorraine, which it had

Below: France mobilised quickly, and, on Saturday afternoon on 1 August 1914, reservists leave the Gare du Nord in Paris for an army centre for kitting out. Each man carries a sack for his personal belongings and civilian clothes, which will be returned when he is in uniform.

lost in the Franco-Prussian War, rather than wait to see what German intentions were and then react. Germany expected the French to do this, and, as with the Belgian border, had developed its rail network in the region to optimise the deployment and supply of its armies. The intention was to lure the French into a trap from where they could be attacked on three sides and the French fell for it, suffering murderously for French Commander-in-Chief Joffre's impetuosity.

It was little better in Belgium, where a 250,000-strong French army met the Germans in battle on 14 August, finally awake to German intentions. After the capture of Brussels on 20 August, Belgium concentrated its forces in Antwerp, ignoring the opportunity to attack the German flank.

By this time the British Expeditionary Force was in France and in good order, and on 23 August met the Germans at Mons just as the Germans started a major drive forward. The British contribution was at this stage a very minor force compared with those of Germany and France, but at Mons they fought hard and well, surprising the Germans with the ferocity and accuracy of their riflemanship. However, it wasn't enough – like the French they fell back and a strategic withdrawal became to all intents and purposes a headlong retreat through France. Mistakes were made on both sides: the Germans failed to rout the BEF despite having opportunities to do so; the Allies for their part withdrew in chaos, and on foot: railways are seldom good at handling unexpected retreats, and the troops marched from their positions on the Belgian border back towards Paris.

Germany's generals were exultant: having inflicted massive casualties on the Allies, particularly the French, they believed victory was near. They abandoned plans to encircle Paris in the expectation that the Allies were beaten and that surrender was a formality. Rather than going around Paris, plans were changed to try and push the French armies out of the way towards Switzerland. With that accomplished,

logic suggested, Paris was theirs for the taking. It was a critical mistake, perhaps the most decisive of the war. When intercepted German radio signals revealed their intentions, Joffre realised that the German advance could be decisively stopped. The Germans, now hundreds of miles beyond their own railheads and still suffering the effects of disruption on Belgium's rail network, were slowing down. German soldiers were exhausted, their horses suffering from a lack of food, and supplies slow to reach them. Having set a blistering pace, the German advance was limited to the speed that soldiers could march and food and ammunition reach the front line. The limitations of using horse-drawn transport to supply armies whose needs were vastly greater than even a generation before were being cruelly exposed – First Army had 84,000 horses needing two *million* pounds of fodder a day – and the German army was approaching its limit. Even so, at the end of August 1914 there was a widespread belief in Germany, as well as in France and London, that the Germans were on the cusp of a great victory.

It was now that both the strengths and weaknesses of railways really began to exert a decisive effect. The Allies had retreated around 150 miles from Mons to the Marne, but as they approached Paris supply lines shortened, communications by telegraph were easier and couldn't be intercepted by the Germans. France could send soldiers to Paris and deploy them by rail to the front, relatively fresh and in good condition, increasingly unlike their opposition. The French rail network was used to switch forces north from Alsace-Lorraine to the centre of the Allied line, an incredibly complex piece of operation at short notice which reflected the capacity and capability of the country's railwaymen. It was the turn of the Allies to go on the offensive.

First came the Battle of the Marne, which was in reality a series of vicious encounters fought along a 100-mile front with both sides on the offensive. The

Right: The 11th Hussars, a British cavalry unit, detraining at Rouen on 18 August 1914. Rouen was a main concentration area for the British Expeditionary Force. Officers in the picture are (left to right): Lieutenants Baggallay, E. Drake and H. Hudson.

Germans were desperately trying to break the French once and for all, the Allies to stem the German advance and go on the counter-attack.

From 6 to 10 September the French – for although the BEF was present they were still vastly outnumbered by their allies and enemies – stopped the Germans. It is often claimed that the use of something like 400 road vehicles ranging from cars and buses to Parisian taxis helped save the day, carrying 4,000 soldiers thirty miles from the outskirts of Paris to the front, yet France's rail network was much more important in keeping troops and supplies flowing. If Germany's mobilisation was a brilliant piece of railway operation, the French operations around Paris were a masterpiece of equal standing and made a decisive contribution to the outcome of the war, which was very much in the balance.

The Germans were weakening, their supply

difficulties growing but as yet they were unbeaten. The French defensive line was precarious, but despite this German High Command convinced itself that its armies were overstretched and should withdraw. Max Hastings suggests that the German Commander-in-Chief, Moltke, had a crisis of nerves, compounded by the inability of General Alexander von Kluck's First Army and Field Marshal Karl von Bülow's Second Army to keep in touch with each other. This opened a gap between them which the BEF began to exploit. Worse still for the Germans, their decision to abandon plans to surround Paris and veer to the south-east seeking a battle of annihilation meant that French General Gallieni was able to attack Kluck's vulnerable flanks. To compound it all, Moltke despatched troops to counter the Russian invasion of East Prussia, though by the time they arrived in the east the Germans had already halted the Russians. A

series of errors and misjudgements by the German generals, and an intelligent retreat and defensive stand by the Allies, halted the Germans. They would never see Paris.

It was one of the key moments of the conflict, and a controversial one, too, as many commentators (and indeed, many German soldiers at the time) believed they had a war-winning advantage over the Allies. It is impossible to say whether the Germans could have fought well for much longer: what it is certain is that they had wrung out their supply lines to the last thread. As long as the French were able to keep formations supplied with fresh soldiers, food, ammunition – and, of course, wine – by rail it was always going to be a near-impossible task for the Germans to defeat them in September 1914, providing morale held up, of course. The Germans retreated to defensive positions above the River Aisne between Compiègne and Berry-au-Bac, and the Allies started to advance, their progress hindered by the destruction of towns, villages and, most crucially of all, railways by the Germans. The Allied advance was a month-long battle – or, more accurately, series of battles – which saw them gradually regain lost territory. The British crossed the Aisne on 12 September but the Germans had the luxury of choosing their defensive positions and inflicted casualties on the British and French whenever and wherever they advanced. The Battle of the Aisne lasted fourteen days and with the growing dominance of artillery and soldiers digging into defensive positions marked the start of the trench warfare for which the Western Front became notorious.

But, despite suffering heavily, the Allies had regained crucial territory, including the vital railhead at Amiens. As we have seen, Amiens' importance to the Allies as a railhead from which to supply armies in northern France was vast, and its recapture a moment of massive importance as far as the railways were concerned.

Opposite page: The story of how fleets of Paris taxis and other road vehicles took soldiers to the front in 1914 has passed into legend – but the railways were much more important.

Above: German Generals Paul von Hindenburg (l.) and Erich Ludendorff were among the architects of the country's military strategy, and pose by a train in Berlin.

From mid-September operations now focused on the almost 200-mile-long gap between the Aisne and the English Channel, flat country in which armies could move easily. The Germans perceived an opportunity to outflank the Allies, while capturing Channel ports such as Calais would cause the Allies huge problems. The British and French were aware of this and, like the Germans, redeployed their forces towards the coast. What is now widely known as the 'Race to the Sea' was a battle fought behind the front

lines, of nations desperately trying to get troops, supplies and reinforcements to where they were needed, stretching rail networks to the limit. Belgium's widespread destruction of its rail network, and the flight of many of its locomotives, carriages and wagons to France, worked heavily against the Germans, who were already struggling to move forces from south to north to beat the Allies to the coast. So extensive was the sabotage that 26,000 labourers were used by the Germans to repair the tracks, but even that huge workforce wasn't able to do the job in time. Even if the railways had been in perfect condition the reality was that there simply weren't enough north–south routes in occupied territory for the Germans to do what they needed.

The Germans didn't help themselves by deciding at this point to attack Antwerp, which the Belgians had fortified as a redoubt. Most of the remaining Belgian army was based there and it became a peculiar irritant to the Germans, who would have been best advised to leave it alone until the British and French had been beaten. Antwerp saw the first major use in the Great War of armoured trains, the first of which employed a 210mm mortar taken from a redoubt. The train was used to protect railways, haul supplies to or from dangerous areas, demolish bridges, and, of course, attack the enemy when the opportunity arose.

The British, so often criticised for their tardiness in France, sent the Royal Naval Division (a force formed of Royal Marine and Royal Navy reservists not needed to serve at sea) to reinforce Antwerp and six 4.7-inch and two 6-inch naval guns brought with them were fitted on armoured trains.

They made little difference: the German assault was determined and strong and by 8 October the

British decided to evacuate their soldiers down the coastal strip. The Royal Naval Division was evacuated from Ostend, but those evacuating included soldiers and civilians alike. It was a predictably chaotic scene, and the last trains were crammed, with every possible refuge taken, even on the roof.

The British left some of their men behind; they were taken prisoner by the Germans, who swiftly despatched them to Germany by train. One of those men was Able Seaman Alf Bastin of Hawke Battalion, Royal Naval Volunteer Reserve, who was captured in Belgium in 1914, who recalled:

> After we were captured, we were put in closed cattle trucks and taken away to Germany. We had nothing to eat for days and we were starving by the time we stopped at Cologne railway station. The Germans had been told that the British Navy had been captured and they wanted to show us off, so they opened up the trucks to public scrutiny. I could see that the platform was crowded with people, mostly women. They just walked along and looked at us, throwing mildewed bread as an insult. This, of course, we were only too glad to eat as we were hungry and we tore off the bits that weren't so mouldy. We were all bewildered, we'd been on the road for three days, then taken on this train and we wondered what the hell we were coming to. They were shouting at us in German, 'Englische Schweinhund!' spitting and swearing and then out of this tumult I heard one voice shout out, very distinctly, 'Englanders, bloody fucking bastards!'

The 'Race to the Sea' ended in a stalemate, with the front line running from the Channel coast to the Swiss border. Casualties so far had been on an unprecedented scale in Europe. On one day alone, 22 August, France lost 27,000 *dead* and many thousands more wounded. Britain and the Commonwealth would spill its share of blood over the coming four years, but it never suffered casualties to that horrific extent.

Both sides had seen hundreds of thousands of men killed or wounded, and neither was strong enough to strike a telling blow. As the Germans regrouped in their defensive lines and the French and British prepared to attack, more soldiers were urgently needed, and Britain now had to recruit, train,

supply and deploy a continental army, something it hadn't anticipated at all.

Above: The demolition of bridges was practised widely on all fronts and by all sides. Whether this locomotive was deliberately driven into the River Marne by retreating forces or the bridge collapsed underneath it, the engineers tasked with retrieving it for repair face a fairly major challenge.

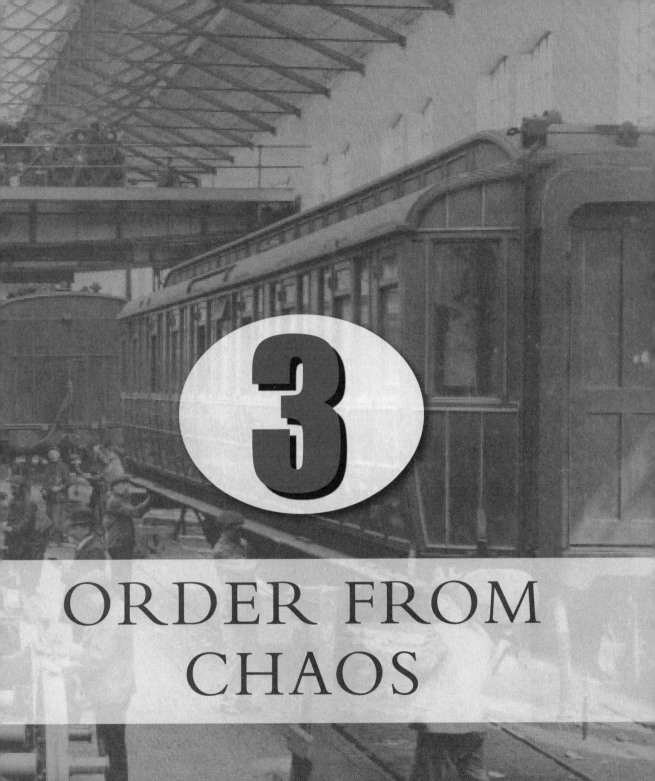

3

ORDER FROM CHAOS

ORDER FROM CHAOS

As 1915 dawned Britain's hopes of a short war had evaporated, and preparations for a lengthy campaign were only just under way. In the nick of time the prospect of total chaos on its transport network was averted – but the railways were under real pressure to deliver.

Britain was in something of a state of shock at the end of 1914. The British Expeditionary Force of 84,000 was reinforced throughout the early stages of the campaign but by the end of 1914 had suffered more than 86,237 casualties killed or wounded, and the quick, decisive war anticipated by all of the combatants was becoming a messy stalemate. Few expected such carnage and, as the wounded came home, 'business as usual', the attitude that had characterised much of 1914, changed to something grimmer and more realistic.

Parliament had called for an additional 100,000 soldiers in August 1914, but as casualties mounted this requirement was raised to 3.5 million men and a massive recruitment drive was mounted. At the time conscription into the services was not regarded as politically acceptable; 750,000 men had joined up by the end of September 1914, and by the end of January 1915 that figure had reached a million. The machinery for fighting a massive continental war was rapidly developing, but Britain was still largely unprepared for the industrial and social pressures this would impose.

The epicentre of Britain's war effort was London – perhaps the most important city in the world at the time and the beating heart of the Empire. And it was spectacular – a vibrant and dynamic demonstration of political, cultural and industrial might. As the war gathered pace, London changed in its appearance and its composition. Pre-war posters advertising products and entertainment for a growing consumer society had by 1915, largely changed in favour of increasingly strident calls for young men: join the army. The posters were highly emotive, using appeals to patriotism, the plight of Belgium and peer pressure. What will your friends think of you if they join up and you don't, the posters asked.

A RAIL REALITY CHECK

Not surprisingly, Britain found its railways under growing pressure. By far the most important form of transportation in the country, the railways carried virtually all of the country's goods, and the majority of passenger traffic, too. They had by and large performed well with the embarkation of the British

THERE IS STILL A PLACE IN THE LINE FOR **YOU**

THIS SPACE IS RESERVED FOR A FIT MAN

Will you fill it?

Left: Britain's railway stations were plastered with advertising before the war, but the advertisements changed dramatically after 1914, with ever more accusatory recruiting posters such as this becoming part of the scene.

Expeditionary Force to France, but with wartime traffic growing rapidly as Britain started to mobilise for a continental war it had never planned for, the strain was beginning to tell.

Raw statistics suggested that Britain's rail network was well placed to cope with wartime demands. With more locomotives, carriages and wagons per route mile and a greater percentage of double-track routes than any other country in Europe, on the face of it the system should have easily had the capacity to handle additional demands. But the statistics masked some fundamental problems.

The first was that there had been no strategic planning of the network: in the *laissez-faire* Victorian age anyone who wanted to build a railway could do so provided they could raise funds and win parliamentary approval. The motive for building the railways was profit for the shareholders rather than any grand plan based on national utility. It meant that routes which looked useful on a map – the Didcot, Newbury & Southampton Railway, for example, which should have provided a really important link to the South Coast from the North without having to approach London - were single-track branch lines with slow speeds and limited capacity. Another good case in point was the Highland Railway from Perth to Thurso. Local traffic was minimal, but, with the Grand Fleet based at Scapa Flow, this single-track route assumed a huge strategic importance that wasn't considered when it was built. There was widespread duplication of routes – often, by accident and of huge benefit to the country. But the lack of coher-

Left: By September 1915 the call to buy war bonds and to join up were becoming ever more strident as the needs of the war grew – but railways such as the Great Central still found space to advertise holiday resorts, new housing developments – and their restaurant car services.

ent planning meant that often where major facilities were really needed they were hopelessly inadequate.

Britain's main lines – the long-distance arteries that could carry the most traffic – were overwhelmingly centred on London. And London has always been a bit of a problem in railway terms. Victorian decisions not to allow railways to penetrate the sanctity of the City of London meant that the main stations and goods facilities were spread out in a ring around the capital and there wasn't any easy way of going through the city.

London's growing underground network would play a crucial role, but not from the point of view of moving troops on, say, the Circle Line from Paddington to King's Cross. From the first day of the conflict the Metropolitan Railway's 'Widened Lines' from Faringdon Street, Holborn, Ludgate Hill and across the Thames through to Loughborough Junction on the South Eastern & Chatham Railway, whose tracks led to the vital port of Dover, provided a vital link from the Great Northern and Midland railways at King's Cross and St Pancras. Although the railway historian J. A. B. Hamilton acknowledged that it was never built to take the volumes of traffic experienced in the war, he calculated that the line conveyed 26,047 troop trains from 5 August 1914 to 31 December 1918 and an unknown but even greater number of goods trains. Hamilton quotes 2,935 passing across the Thames in the first two weeks of February 1915. Operational restrictions included the banking of trains and the limitation of goods trains to just twenty-five loaded wagons but the ability to travel from north to south London without extensive and slow deviations was vital.

On the other side of London a vital connection was the North London line from Poplar and the docks across to the London & North Western Railway lines at Willesden and then a connection with the London & South Western Railway (LSWR), enabling a connection across the Thames which saw 13,565 military specials during the war.

These links in London were critical but the other big problem was that the railways simply weren't set up to handle large additional movements of troops and military supplies. There were no extensive embarkation facilities like those the Germans had set up; there wasn't a pool of carriages and wagons that could readily be dedicated to military needs – there was simply no financial incentive for the railway companies to do that. Unlike the railways of most of its European counterparts, Britain's civilian railway would have to adapt within the means at its disposal in 1914.

The final headache the railways posed was one of fragmentation. There were hundreds of railway companies, with many smaller operations running tiny country byways and a few regional giants operating the country's main lines. Even before the war planning a journey from one side of the country to the other could be a mind-bogglingly complex exercise with myriad choices of services and a bewildering array of fares and journey times, which could often be very, very different. This fragmentation applied to almost every aspect of railway operation. The locomotives varied wildly in age, performance and reliability. The best of the best in the early twentieth century stood comparison with anything in Europe, but a short walk from Birmingham's Snow Hill station to New Street would have showcased the differences in

Left: The Grimsby Chums had many railwaymen among their numbers – but there was still an air of enthusiastic amateurism during their training, despite them being issued with modern Lee-Enfield .303 rifles.

PROTECTING THE RAILWAY

At the outbreak of war there were real concerns about German saboteurs damaging the rail network, and sentries were posted at key structures such as the Severn Tunnel and Royal Albert Bridge near Plymouth to guard the line. The idea made a degree of sense but it soon became clear that the sentries were more of a danger than the enemy. Track gangers took their lives in their hands when they approached sentries (after all, it was the perfect cover for any potential saboteur) and when the weather closed in and at night, the sound of approaching footsteps invariably made the soldiers nervous. After fourteen were hit by trains and another two shot their reliefs, the plan was modified.

In Britain ad hoc volunteer forces were organised in November 1914 to become the Central Association of Volunteer Training Corps, and had to be self-supporting financially, provide their own uniforms (which could not be khaki to prevent confusion with the Army), and all members had to wear an armband or brassard of 'GR' for Georgius Rex. These units were open to those who had genuine reasons for not enlisting in the regular armed forces – such as many railwaymen – and although known as 'George's Wrecks' or 'Grandpa's Regiment' by sceptics, performed a valuable role in guarding vulnerable points, munitions handling, digging defences and assisting with harvests and firefighting amongst other activities. They presaged in many ways the formation of the Home Guard in the Second World War and played a valuable and often overlooked role in home defence in Britain.

stark form. Facilities for passengers taken for granted by most a generation later, such as lavatories and corridors connecting coaches in a train, were far from universal; even technical details such as braking systems and signalling were almost always completely different from one railway to another. It was a massive duplication of effort that was, in truth, only just affordable before 1914: in wartime it was not. It could have been – and very nearly was – a recipe for an uncoordinated, chaotic mess.

That it was not was down to the eleventh-hour creation of a national managing committee to try and

SPECIAL RAILWAY NOTICE

PACKAGES

tendered for conveyance

BY

PASSENGER TRAIN

OWING TO THE LARGE NUMBER OF RAILWAYMEN WHO HAVE ENLISTED, AND THE CONSEQUENT SHORTAGE OF STAFF, TRADERS AND OTHERS ARE REQUESTED NOT TO FORWARD BY PASSENGER TRAIN ANY PACKAGE WEIGHING MORE THAN 3 CWT.

By Order of the

RAILWAY EXECUTIVE COMMITTEE.

London, June 1915.

impose some semblance of order on the chaos. For decades successive governments had half-heartedly investigated ways of coordinating railways at times of crisis but it wasn't until 1911 that the German threat started to be considered. The question asked at the time was how London could be supplied with food, goods and raw materials if enemy action closed the North Sea ports, which sent a lot of coastal shipping to the capital. The answer was a committee formed of the General Managers of the railways concerned to jointly manage their efforts under the provisions of the Regulation of the Forces Act, 1871, which allowed the government effectively to take control of the railways. A year later, expanded from the initial six railways to the biggest ten, it met for the first time. Under the leadership of the Acting Chairman – effectively working as a deputy for the President of the Board of Trade – the Railway Executive Committee (REC) had sweeping powers to decide operational priorities and manage the railways as a national system. Britain had been lucky to stumble on a structure that allowed the railway companies to retain a degree of independence but still operating under national control in the nick of time. It was also lucky, to an extraordinary degree, that the General Managers of the major railways represented on the REC were among the best the country ever produced. Other personalities may have put their own company's vested interests first, leading to endless squabbles, but with the likes of the London & South Western Railway's Herbert Walker (whose company would bear much of the brunt of troop embarkations) there were just about enough genuine experts to keep the trains moving.

TAKING IT SERIOUSLY?

The odd thing was that through much of the last half of 1914 a casual observer might not realise from looking at the railways that there was a war on at all. Most passenger trains ran to their usual schedules,

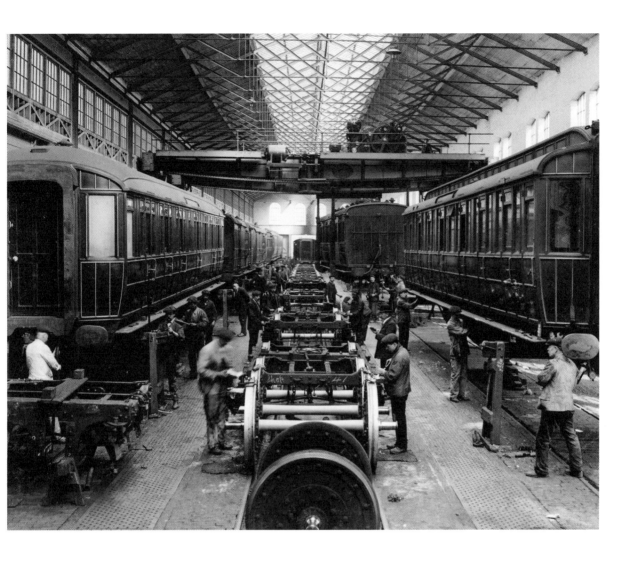

excursion trains still ran, and some trains were even accelerated despite rising volumes of military traffic. It was a little odd as the net revenue of the railway companies was capped at 1913/14 levels for the duration of the war – there was no incentive for the railway companies to try and meet the demand, but with the expectation of a short war they seemed to feel bound to do so.

It is too simplistic to blame the railways for carrying on as normal, however. Rising wages – increased by a shortage of labour as men joined up and were

Opposite: As wartime demands on the railway grew and men enlisted, the Railway Executive Committee tried to dampen demand for services hitherto taken for granted. Their early efforts were only partially successful.

Above: Railway works such as the Great Northern's huge Doncaster site were at full stretch with additional military manufacturing, but maintenance and repair of locomotives, carriages and wagons had to continue. This photograph shows bogies being repaired in the West Carriage Shop.

later conscripted into the armed forces – meant that many people could afford to travel by train for the first time and they began to do so in great numbers. How does a democratic society that places a high value on individual freedom such as Britain deal with such demand? Even when fares were raised by 50 per cent in 1917 some of the larger railway companies reported passenger numbers *still* increasing 40 per cent year on year. Restricting individual rights of travel would be difficult if not impossible to manage even if it were desirable; traffic levels couldn't be increased at the expense of military services, and the only other option, a massive rise in fares to try and choke off demand, was, as we have seen, unsuccessful as well as politically undesirable. Right until the end of the war the increased ability and desire of the general public to travel posed an operational headache that was never really resolved.

CHANGING THE PATTERN

Things really started to change in 1915, with greater traffic levels finally forcing the REC's hand and seeing service reductions. In February 180 trains on competing routes were cut, as were many dining-car and some sleeping-car facilities. A raft of cheap fares to the likes of football matches, race meetings and so on were scrapped (though there were, as J. A. B. Hamilton notes, many exceptions) – but it was the East Coast routes from London to York, Newcastle and Edinburgh which were hit hardest. The growing threat of Germany's High Seas Fleet to the North Sea ports prompted a massive shift of coal traffic from coastal shipping to the railway. As with all of the

Right: *The big change in the railway works was the introduction of women on the shop floor. While the big skilled jobs remained the preserve of men, production of fittings for carriages was considered suitable for females, and thousands found employment in places such as Doncaster Works.*

industrialised world, Britain was fuelled by coal, and without coal the factories would stop and the lights literally go out. It had to take priority over almost everything else.

With major operating bottlenecks at Peterborough, Huntingdon, Sandy, Welwyn and Hadley Wood, the Great Northern Railway was struggling to cope with traffic levels before the war, and now the additional military and coal traffic brought huge delays to the East Coast Main Line. The big problem with goods trains was that their speeds varied so much. The fastest could manage 45mph but the slowest plodded along at 20mph. Slow trains had to be held in passing loops to allow faster ones to pass. Journey times were extended and scarce track capacity squandered. The GNR took what even today looks like a very brave decision to reduce the maximum speed of all goods trains to 20mph and increase their length to eighty wagons irrespective of the type of traffic. It then went a step further and ran coal trains to Ferme Park and goods trains to Hornsey in strict alternating pattern. It solved, just in time, the complete blockage of one of Britain's most important routes, which served stations and industries all the way up to the Highlands of Scotland. Without any overt political pressure or instruction, intelligent railway management was saving the day.

SERVING THE SOUTH

Although sending troops via Dover to France was fairly straightforward and logical, the military recognised that it would have to spread the load. It had long planned to use Southampton as a major embarkation point for troops heading to Europe and as early as August 1914 it was designated Military Embarkation Port No. 1 – an importance it retained through the war. Southampton's docks were expanded massively in the late nineteenth and early twentieth centuries, and were actually owned by the London & South Western Railway. The expansion to cater for growing ocean

liner traffic served the country well, providing the port with the ability to handle thousands of people every day. It was the Edwardian equivalent of Heathrow Airport – the country's most important and capable civilian port – and its facilities would prove crucial in keeping troops and supplies flowing to the front.

Whereas Southampton and the LSWR were the focal point for the BEF embarkation and had

Previous page: The demand for horses and mules on the front lines was significant and they were carried by train and ship to France. These horses are being loaded on to a train at Ormskirk, Lancs, on 11 December 1914.

Above: Southampton Docks was the Heathrow Airport of its day with a vast network of railways feeding the quays, for passenger and freight traffic. The huge number of wagons comprised a workload that would scarcely be reduced until the 1950s.

THE WAVERLEY LINE AND STOBS MILITARY AND POW CAMP – A CHILDHOOD MEMORY

High up on the bleak moorland of the Cheviot Hills near Hawick in Scotland the construction in 1903 of a military camp at Stobs saw a siding laid to serve it at the station on the North British Railway route from Edinburgh to Carlisle.

The first troops began their training at Stobs that summer and by the end of July more than 20,000 men had used the facilities. After the declaration of war in August 1914 Stobs camp assumed greater importance as Kitchener's army of volunteers and partially trained Territorial soldiers began arriving by rail from all over the country.

From 1915 the camp was also used for the accommodation of Austrian and Turkish internees and, in increasing numbers, German prisoners of war. A separate camp with more than 200 huts capable of holding up to 6,000 men was constructed during the year. On completion the civilian internees were moved elsewhere. As the Geneva Convention allowed for non-commissioned officers and other ranks to be employed in manual labour tasks the prisoners were given building and labouring jobs around the camp and also on the local farms, replacing the local men who had joined up.

Since its inception, and because of its proximity to Stobs railway station, the camp had also seen many civilian visitors – particularly young women and girls – to visit their men in training with the many Scottish regiments on their Sundays off. After August 1914 the numbers of these visitors increased and in later years, as the POWs themselves became more numerous, were further swelled by sightseers drawn to view the enemy in the flesh. Stobs station was busy with troops arriving and departing, the delivery of mail, building materials, army stores and an unprecedented number of Sunday visitors for the camp. The latter increased by such a degree that in July 1915 an Exclusion Order was implemented to prevent civilians entering the camp unless issued with a pass.

A young Border girl, Elsie Elliot, was one of the many visitors to Stobs in those years, visiting family and friends at one of the local farms, and also to Hawick, the birthplace of her mother. She recalled travelling on the North British Railway trains from the south up to Stobs and remembered the camp, its barbed wire and the awe she felt at seeing real live German soldiers just beyond it. She remembered talking 'through the wire' to some of the men who spoke English. One of these men who worked on a local farm made her a wooden doll with painted clothes that she cherished. 1919 saw the last of the prisoners leave to return home and to Elsie's regret she never kept the name of the man who had shown her such kindness.

Further south on the Waverley line, beyond Riccarton and on towards Kershopefoot, Elsie recalled tales of local young men and the pressure of volunteering for war service, and, after early 1916, the very real fear of conscription. Many men from this area of Eskdale, Liddisdale and Teviotdale hid in this remote, but to them, familiar hinterland in an attempt to escape the clutches of the military. Some of these 'draft dodgers' met local sympathisers who had prepared food parcels and other essential supplies for them. Another method was to drop off similar parcels along the route of the Waverley line at remote prearranged points for collection. No names were ever mentioned in the telling of these exploits and there was never any hint that the railway company staff were (officially, anyway) aware of the goings-on: even after the war a stigma would have been attached to the men. But although such stories have the resonance of the many tales of the Border reivers and their deeds of derring-do, they remain no more than anecdotal. Knowing Elsie as I did as her son, I suspect there's more than a little truth sitting just behind the romance.
— *Railway author Nick Deacon*

a few days' notice to prepare, the South Eastern & Chatham Railway, which served south-east England, was in the firing line from the very first day of the war with the arrival of thousands of refugees caught by the rapid German advance and fleeing from the French and Belgian ports across to the port of Folkestone. On one day 6,000 refugees were landed from Ostend alone, many of them arriving with just the clothes they stood in. The SECR had to deal with the problem of feeding them, finding temporary shelter and then getting them away from the coast to more permanent accommodation. The port of Dover was exclusively taken over by the naval and military authorities and three SECR steamers were also requisitioned for use by the Royal Navy.

At Ashford Works the company had to start immediately on a programme of replacement parts for Belgian and French locomotives which had lost the use of servicing depots overrun by German forces. As with all the major railway works in Britain, Ashford had a complete manufacturing capability, able to make everything from a door handle to a complete locomotive, and these skills would be used to the fullest throughout the conflict at works such as Crewe, Swindon, Derby, Doncaster, York, Darlington, Horwich and others, making ammunition (including gas shells later in the conflict), components for guns, and almost everything else the military might require – in addition to their own railway needs.

Dover Marine station, unfinished at the start of the war, was hurriedly completed and, along with Southampton, selected for the reception of steamers conveying sick and wounded from the front. During the war an average of three ambulance steamers arrived at the port with 1,250,000 sick and wounded servicemen. In addition, leave and draft sailings accounted for the passage of a further 1,750,000 men.

Special munitions services were run from Woolwich Arsenal to Richborough Military Port in Kent formed of wooden box trucks from the marshalling yards at Hither Green. A total of 101,872 of these trains were run during the war or an average of sixty-six trains per day. Richborough Military Port was opened in 1916 to send heavy equipment for the BEF to France and from 1918 even operated roll-on, roll-off train ferries, the first time these ships had been used in Britain.

The role of the SECR – whose routes from London were short but critical – was summed up in a letter written by Douglas Haig at the conclusion of the war to SECR Chairman Cosmo Bonsor:

> *We have been more closely associated with the South Eastern & Chatham Railway than any other. The bulk of our ammunition and stores required for the maintenance of our armies, as well as several millions of men as reinforcements and on leave, have passed over their system. Their sphere of duty, too, has been nearest to the shores of France and Belgium, and consequently more open to hostile attacks by air and fears of invasion. The traffic for the Armies in France has never ceased to flow. This reflects the greatest credit on all concerned with the Company.*

For those soldiers sailing from Southampton, Dover and the other embarkation points, however, the glitz, gloss and glamour of pre-war ocean crossing had little relevance to their voyage to the French ports: troopships may have been passenger vessels pre-war but in conflict they were strictly utilitarian. The need was to get as many soldiers and their equipment across the Channel as possible, and quickly.

For those heading to Dover or Richborough, a train from Victoria was likely to be the way to the front, but Southampton, that much further west from London, had options. Many travelled from London along the LSWR's main line, and others still used the link from the key Great Western Railway junction at

Reading to reach the port via Basingstoke. Two other routes to the south from the Midlands and beyond also played a role beyond anything expected of them pre-war and, although they weren't built as main lines and couldn't carry anything like the loads of the Basingstoke to Southampton line, they assumed an importance far beyond their peacetime remit.

The most important of these was the Midland & South Western Junction Railway (MSWJR). Connecting the Midland Railway's network at Cheltenham with the LSWR's at Andover, it provided a north–south link which bypassed the busy railways around London at a distance. Substantial parts of it had been doubled in response to growing traffic which aided timekeeping and increased capacity. The military first started paying attention to it from 1905 when a much enlarged army camp opened at Tidworth on Salisbury Plain, served by a branch line from Ludgershall. The camp had extensive barracks blocks for cavalry and infantry units with extensive stores and stabling connected internally by a private military railway. This was connected to the MSWJR through interchange sidings at the terminus of Tidworth station. It was already an important conduit for military traffic prior to the war, and assumed a greater role on the outbreak of war with Salisbury Plain, one of the main areas for troop concentrations and their subsequent movement to Southampton for embarkation to France. As the Allied commitment grew and from 1918 American soldiers demanded transportation to France from Glasgow and Liverpool, the MSWJR gained further importance. By the end of the war it had carried 6,452 troop trains, 1,488 ambulance trains, and hauled 134,852 horses, 9,021 ammunition wagons, 8,717 artillery pieces and 15,176 tons of baggage. For a railway neither built nor intended as a main line, these were impressive figures indeed.

The other route, the Didcot, Newbury and Southampton (DNS), ran from Didcot to Southampton via Newbury and linked the east–west main lines of the Great Western Railway and the LSWR. The camp at Churn, high up on the Berkshire Downs, provided military traffic but the establishment of a large Royal Army Ordnance Corps depot at Didcot meant that this little single-track railway justified its purpose. Other camps were established along the route to benefit from its easy access to Southampton. With a greater strategic vision along German policy lines, these railways would almost certainly have been expanded and improved before the war, and, in the Second World War, the DNS was indeed doubled to carry vital traffic ahead of the D-Day landings.

It wasn't just soldiers embarking for the front who passed through Southampton; the wounded returning to Britain received further treatment at hospitals around the country and a fleet of ambulance trains took them from the hospital ships to their destination. Britain's railways proved remarkably adept at creating ambulance trains for domestic use. Spurred on by experiences of the Boer War where the Red Cross-funded 'Princess Christian' train had proved highly successful, the London and North Western Railway was tasked with designing a standard ambulance train suitable for use all over Britain; when war was declared the War Office ordered an initial twelve, to be built by seven of the largest railways. The first arrived at Southampton just hours too late to take the first batch of wounded soldiers on 24 August 1914 – a demonstration of the railways' ability to act quickly on pre-prepared plans.

On the home front, Britain's railways – as disorganised and as chaotic as they were pre-war – were by 1915 starting to work effectively and in partnership to support the nation. But traffic levels were rising and the pressures were building: they were about to give way in tragic fashion.

PRINCIPAL RAILWAYS IN BRITAIN, C.1914

Thurso
Wick
Peterhead
Kyle of Lochalsh
Aberdeen
Mallaig
Inverness
Dundee
Oban
Perth
Glasgow
Edinburgh
Berwick
Stranraer
Quintinshill
Newcastle
Carlisle
Middlesborough
Barrow
York
Liverpool
Manchester
Doncaster
Grimsby
Holyhead
Newark
Crewe
Derby
Aberystwyth
Birmingham
Rugby
Norwich
Worcester
Peterborough
Cambridge
Fishguard
Gloucester
Oxford
Ipswich
Harwich
Swansea
Didcot
LONDON
Bristol
Basingstoke
Dover
Taunton
Southampton
Portsmouth
Exeter
Weymouth
Plymouth
Falmouth

LSWR Main Line
West Coast Main Line
East Coast Main Line
Highland Main Line
SECR Main Line
Didcot, Newbury and Southampton Railway
Midland and South Western Junction Railway

100 miles
100km

PREPARED ITALY

Since 1882 Italy had been allied with Germany and Austria but had found it increasingly expedient also to maintain close ties with France, Britain and Russia. In July 1914, with the threat of war drawing closer, Italy began preparing for war against France in accordance with its treaty with the Central Powers. However, the terms of the agreement stated that Italy was only bound to defend its allies if one of them was attacked first. The Austrian ultimatum to Serbia was seen by the Italians as an act of aggression and offered a loophole through which a grateful Italy was freed of its treaty obligations and could declare itself officially neutral.

This was clearly a popular move within the country given the bitter rivalry with Austria over an area of the South Tyrol running down from the mountainous Trentino region to the coastal plain known as the Austrian Littoral lying west of Slovenia. Crucially for Austrian interests, the coastal area also contained Trieste, her one primary seaport and an area known as the Austrian Riviera.

After the myth of German invincibility had been shattered on the Marne in September 1914 and the Russian advance into Austrian Galicia, it appeared that victory for the Entente powers was highly likely and Italy's continued stance of neutrality began to waver.

By April 1915, Italy had now placed itself within the Entente camp and, sweetened by the promise of rich territorial gains that would result from the defeat of Austria and the breakup of its empire, had now firmly committed itself to the opening of a new front along its northern and easterly boundary with Austria.

However, despite the promises of the Treaty of London, a difficult war still had to be won and many within the Italian government were both pessimistic and uncertain. As if reflecting this mood, popular reaction to the eventual declaration of war on 23 May hardly resembled the scenes of jingoistic fervour that had accompanied the same declarations in Britain, France and Russia.

Militarily, Italy was fresh from a demoralising war with the Ottoman Empire over the possession of Libya and had been caught unawares by its unexpected cost in financial terms and casualties suffered. Losses in personnel and *matériel* in this conflict had not been replaced and continued insurrections against Italian rule continued to tie troops down in Libya.

For the impending campaign the main (and obvious) areas of conflict with the Austrians were the daunting Alpine regions of the Tyrol and the easily defended valleys of the Isonzo and Vipava valleys. Although the Italian army could initially field some 549 battalions against a numerically inferior Austrian army, the most critical factor was that it faced an enemy experienced in recent modern warfare. Furthermore, this was an army equipped with the latest artillery and machine guns and in possession of some of the most natural and dominating defensive positions known to man. By contrast, the Italian army, weak in artillery and logistical muscle, could initially offer only the dash and elan of its troops against mountain redoubts, modern firepower and barbed-wire entanglements up to 40ft thick.

The supply position was uninviting for the Italians. Although Italy was now benefiting from the 1905 state acquisition of its private railway companies, there were only two railways running towards the Austrian border – one northwards from a junction at Verona through the Trentino valley to Innsbruck and the other from Bologna to Udine. Beyond the pitifully few railheads spurred from the course of these lines the army would need to rely on the age-old method of mule trains until the Fiat motor company of Turin could turn out quantities of trucks robust enough to carry men and supplies along the tortuous roads up to the front.

It was not an inviting prospect but, as if to emphasise the importance of the region, it was said

that the Tyrol frontier was worth three victorious campaigns to the Austrians. The next three years of conflict in this area would more than prove the point.

Above: The Italian painter Achille Beltrame – and co-originator of weekly illustrated newspaper La Domenica del Corriere *– painted many illustrations of the war in Italy, and this painting purports to show Italian naval staff manning an armoured train patrolling the Adriatic coastline to protect against Austro-Hungarian attacks. It has been suggested, however, that the painting may be based on photographs of Belgian armoured trains of 1914 – if true, then this atmospheric image is a classic case of artistic licence being used in wartime to convey a suitably patriotic message.*

4

A SHOCK TO
THE SYSTEM

A SHOCK TO THE SYSTEM

With traffic on Britain's railways rising, the loss of 8 per cent of their workforce to the armed forces added to the strains of a system never built to cope with the loads as summer 1915 approached. But was Britain's worst ever railway accident a result of the pressure, or of simple human fallibility?

The huge numbers of men enlisting affected the railways hugely, with 55,000 joining up by the end of 1914, 8 per cent of their combined pre-war staff. Although many posts were perhaps less than essential (labour was cheap and all but the smallest stations given a full complement of staff), when young, fit men from the operating departments joined up it created a staff shortage and added to the pressures on an already hard-pressed network.

To alleviate this in March 1915 the Railway Executive Committee outlined plans to replace men in non-essential (which in practice meant 'skilled') jobs with women. In August 1914 the railways already employed 13,046 women but by the end of the war there were 68,000, from engine cleaners, carriage and wagon cleaners to porters and clerks. By the end of 1915, 100,000 railwaymen had joined the colours, exacerbating the labour shortage and increasing the need for women to work on the railways. Having, like so many industries, denigrated the role and ability of women to perform as well as men, Britain's railways now depended utterly on their overlooked efforts.

One of those railwaymen who joined up was a nineteen-year-old clerk at the Glasgow and South Western Railway's Nitshill station near Glasgow called John Meikle. A highly regarded student and keen footballer, had the war not intervened he had started on a career that, in time, might have led to him becoming a station manager. He was a typical example of how the railways of the time could and did pick the very best the working classes had to offer – whether station clerks or engine cleaners, fitters or firemen, the calibre of the railways' younger staff made it inevitable that many would join up despite a decision being made early on that many roles on

Right: One of the most visible roles of women on Britain's wartime railways was in cleaning locomotives and carriages – jobs usually done by younger men before the war. This Great Central Railway Class 11B 4-4-0 positively sparkles thanks to their efforts – a remarkable achievement in wartime conditions.

the railway would be exempt from military service because of their importance to the wider war effort.

Meikle tried repeatedly to join the army but was rejected each time. His mother reckoned that his chest measurements were too small, but through persistence and by lying about his age he finally managed to enlist in February 1915 and started his training at Maryhill Barracks, Glasgow, where he joined the Fourth Battalion, Seaforth Highlanders. His training took him first to Bedford in England before continuing at Fort George, near Inverness. On his journey north he would have travelled over the Highland Railway from Perth to Fort George, a route already stretched to its limits. Its main line ran for 272 miles from Perth to Thurso and was largely single-track, with some short sections of double-track over the steepest inclines. The decision taken in 1905 to base the Royal Navy's Grand Fleet at Scapa Flow in the Orkney Islands was to make massive demands of the route that had not been anticipated when it was built. It carried seamen and naval staff to Thurso, the nearest mainland port to Scapa (though coal for the battleships was sent to Grangemouth and shipped from there), huge quantities of timber south (much of it for pit props or, heading in the opposite direction, for building the defences at Scapa), and considerable local coal traffic to replace coastal shipping. It was like threading a rope through a needle and here, perhaps before anywhere else on the rail network, the strain really showed.

Within a year around 100 of the Highland Railway's 152 locomotives were worn out or run down, and the Railway Executive Committee arranged for

Left: The Highland Railway had a very distinctive look, which it retained through to the 1950s. Although this image was taken post-war, when the company was part of the London Midland & Scottish Railway, the 'Loch' 4-4-0 epitomises the daintiness of much of the railway's fleet. Perth was much busier than the majority of the company's other stations.

a motley fleet of replacements from railways all over Britain. Many were obsolescent already but they kept the trains running – it was providing the staff that proved a bigger headache for the Highland and other railways. Twelve- or even fourteen-hour days were common, not helped by the inevitable operating delays on this overstretched railway. Working weeks of up to seventy hours for the locomotive crews were common – if anyone had been cynical enough to wager where an accident might happen, the Highland Railway looked a good bet.

DISASTER AT QUINTINSHILL

However, it was further south in May 1915 that the railway apparently cracked from the relentless pressures of operating under the conditions of total war. On 22 May 1915 a twenty-one-vehicle troop train with fifteen coaches was carrying 500 soldiers from the Territorial 1/7 Leith Battalion, The Royal Scots, from Larbert, near Falkirk, to Liverpool, from where they were due to embark for Gallipoli.

The soldiers were being sent to join the offensive at Gallipoli, a daring bid to force open the Black Sea to Russia and knock the Ottoman Empire out of the war. For most if not all it would be their first action, and on the train there must have been an intense mixture of nerves, apprehension and fear combined with excitement about potentially playing a decisive role in the conflict as they headed south that morning. Those soldiers who could slept, conserving their energies for the battles ahead. Others would have spent their time reading, or talking with their comrades, or playing cards on what was to be a long journey to the front line.

They were travelling on the West Coast Main Line, which runs for 399 miles from London to Glas-

Right: The 1/5th Battalion, Seaforth Highlanders, departs from Wick on 6 August 1914 on the Highland Railway. At one of the northern extremities of Britain's rail network, their journey was definitely southbound!

DEPARTURE of TERRITORIAL FORCES
WICK 6TH AUG. 1914.

gow, serving many of Britain's most important cities either directly or on connecting routes, including Birmingham, Manchester and Liverpool. It was Britain's busiest and most important railway, carrying vast volumes of passenger and goods traffic even in peacetime. In wartime the loads intensified with military traffic adding to the workload of hard-pressed engine crews, track gangs, and two signalmen in a signalbox at Quintinshill, near Gretna Green – though the timetable planners were well aware of the West Coast Main Line's capacity and the trains running at the time were well within that.

For three years Signalmen George Meakin and James Tinsley had changed over from the night to the day shift at 6.30 a.m. instead of the 6 a.m. they were supposed to. This was to save a 1½-mile walk from Gretna and allowed the man starting the day shift to ride the local Carlisle–Beattock train as far as Quintinshill if it were due to be held there. The signalman on the night shift wrote down the signalling movements he'd done in the extra half-hour and then his replacement filled in the train register which keeps a record of all train movements in the area. Whether Meakin was overtired or simply distracted by Tinsley in the signalbox is unclear, but a series of decisions taken by the pair of them would prove fatal.

The first move had been to hold the 0450 goods train from Carlisle in one of the loop lines built to allow faster trains to overtake. Meakin then had a problem, though: the 0610 Carlisle–Beattock local train was due, but so were a pair of late running express sleeper trains from London to the North. If he let

Previous page: The devastation at Quintinshill was total. Only the burned-out frames of the carriages remain.

Right: Firemen play their hoses on the tender of 'Cardean' 4-6-0 No. 907, which hauled the local train involved in the crash. Although the carriages burned out quickly, locomotive coal continued to burn long afterwards. The locomotive was beyond repair and was scrapped in January 1916.

the local train continue it would delay the express- es further, so he had to shunt it out of the way. The only way he could do this was to reverse the train on to the southbound line and then let it resume its journey once the express had passed. Even though it meant that the local train was potentially in the path of the troop train, the signalling system would, if operated correctly, prevent any trains from entering the same track space, known as a 'section'.

However, Meakin failed to tell the signalbox at Kirkpatrick, just under three miles north of Quintinshill, that the southbound line was occupied and not to send any trains towards Quintinshill until he was given the all-clear. This was done by a simple bell code sent via telegraph wires and the procedures were absolute: a train could only enter the section of track ahead if the signalman at the next signalbox down the line confirmed that the route was clear. If

Above: Injured soldiers receive first aid in a field soon after the accident.

AN EYEWITNESS ACCOUNT OF QUINTINSHILL

' *I travelled in the third or fourth compartment of the first carriage from the engine of the troop train and the first I knew of anything being wrong was when awakened by the shock of the collision and I found myself falling down with glass and water falling about me. There was a short space and then a second shock …*

I did not notice fire at first and I think I went to the rear end of the train without noticing much. I stayed there for some time and I then saw an engine and two or three carriages piled up, and fire was rising from them. The battalion tool coach was on the train and the tools were got out of it and employed on, I think, the roof of a sleeping saloon car. One lady was got out after the roof was cut off. So far as I saw there were more tools than men using them. '

Lieutenant J. C. Bell, 1/7 Royal Scots

WOMEN ON THE RAILWAYS

Men overwhelmingly dominated the railways of
Europe, as they did so many industries at the time.
True, women worked in all railways in traditional
roles such as secretaries, and in restaurants, cafés
and hotels – something like 13,000 were employed in such jobs in Britain alone – but many
roles were the preserve of men only.

The drain of manpower to the forces led
all sides to employ women on their railways in
greater numbers. In Britain from 1915 passengers
saw for the first time women collecting and issu-
ing tickets and acting as porters. Women cleaned
engines and carriages. Women even worked in
the big locomotive works on semi-skilled manufacturing jobs, but the most specialised roles
in engineering – and of driving and firing the
trains – were denied them. This wasn't simple
discrimination – it reflected the fact that extensive
training was needed to do these jobs safely and
effectively – but there were concerns, too, that the
physical demands would be beyond most ladies.

Fifty-six thousand women were employed,
but they were not given a warm welcome: there
were fears that when the war was over men who
survived would find their jobs taken by women,
and the companies had to guarantee that the jobs
were 'hostilities-only' appointments.

It would be a cliché to suggest that all women
employed by the railways enjoyed their work or
that they found it liberating: as with the menfolk,
many did not. It certainly wasn't the driving force
behind the suffragette movement, but in proving
that women could do jobs hitherto denied them
as well as men, one of the fundamental objections
to employing them was removed.

From 1914 to 1918 the railways of Europe
could not have operated as successfully as they did
without the contribution and dedication of many
thousands of women.

it was occupied, the train would have to wait. The
fireman of the local train was also supposed to visit
the signalbox in such circumstances to remind the
signalman that his train was facing the wrong way on
the southbound line and to check that a special collar
was fitted to the lever operating the signal north of
the local train to prevent it from being released. He
did neither, and Meakin *hadn't* fitted the signal collar
to prevent the lever being moved.

A southbound special train formed of empty coal
wagons heading from Grangemouth to South Wales
– yet another demand made by the war effort – was
now approaching and signalling into the loop line
on those tracks. By now three of the four tracks at
Quintinshill were occupied – and vital safety meas-
ures still hadn't been undertaken. But despite this, for
the time being all of the trains in the area were in
little danger of accident.

It was at this time, however, that Meakin and
Tinsley were both preoccupied, with Tinsley filling
in the train register to cover his tracks, and Meakin
in charge of the signalbox. For some reason – perhaps
it was the presence of two additional and prohibited
visitors in his signalbox from the goods trains, perhaps
it was tiredness – one of them erroneously signalled
that the southbound coal train (which along with the
local train was standing right in front of them) had
passed out of the section and that the route to Carlisle was clear. The first of the delayed northbound
expresses passed safely at 0638 but the local train was
still standing on the southbound line, again in full
view of the signalbox. Kirkpatrick signalbox asked for
permission to send the troop train towards Quintinshill; Tinsley, as the signalman on duty, should have
refused but didn't – in fact, he inexplicably offered
the train forward to Gretna Junction, a shade under
1½ miles south despite the route being blocked. Had
the protective collar been placed on the signal lever,
Tinsley would never have been able to clear it, and,
although he would have already been in trouble with

TICKET COLLECTOR

the railway authorities for an irresponsible series of errors, it would have been far less than what he set in progress as he pulled the lever to clear his signal.

As far as the driver and firemen of the troop train were concerned the route was clear so they accelerated their train to make up time. With a lengthy downhill gradient they picked up speed quickly, but they had no way of knowing that they were on a collision course with the local train, which was *still* waiting on the southbound main line. Oblivious to his error, Tinsley then compounded it by accepting the other delayed northbound express.

As the troop train approached, the fireman of the local train spotted that the signals which should have been protecting him were cleared for a train. Looking down the main line, the local's driver, David Wallace, spotted the troop train 200 yards away bearing down on him at high speed. He and his fireman, George Hutchinson, leaped for their lives as the collision neared. At 0650 the driver of the troop train, F. Scott, and fireman, J. Hannah, must have looked ahead in horror as they saw the local train on the tracks ahead. They slammed on the brakes and threw the engine into reverse, but with well over 433 tons driving him forward it would have made no difference. The collision was fast, violent and devastating. The wooden-bodied and wooden-chassised coaches carrying the Royal Scots splintered and shattered; wreckage was strewn over the tracks, some of the carriages leaping over the engine in the force of the collision, the tender of their locomotive straddling the northbound line. Such was its force that a train which left Larbert 221 yards long had 'telescoped' into a length of just 67 yards. Dazed and frightened, those survivors able to climb from the carriages did so gingerly

Right: *The funeral of the Quintinshill victims took place on 24 May 1915 in a three-hour procession from the battalion drill hall in Dalmeny Street, Edinburgh, to Rosebank Cemetery on the boundary of Leith and Edinburgh. Four unidentified children from the disaster were buried in Glasgow.*

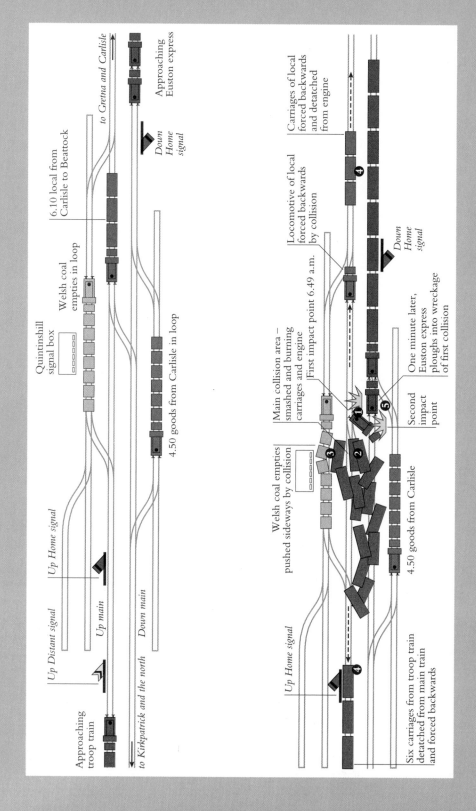

to Gretna and Carlisle

Approaching
Euston express

6.10 local from
Carlisle to Beattock

Down
Home
signal

Quintinshill
signal box

Welsh coal
empties in loop

Carriages of local
forced backwards
and detached
from engine

Locomotive of local
forced backwards
by collision

Down
Home
signal

4.50 goods from Carlisle in loop

Main collision area –
smashed and burning
carriages and engine

First impact point 6.49 a.m.

One minute later,
Euston express
ploughs into wreckage
of first collision

Second
impact
point

Welsh coal empties
pushed sideways by collision

4.50 goods from Carlisle

Up Home signal

Six carriages from troop train
detached from main train
and forced backwards

Up Distant signal

Up Home signal

Up main

Down main

Approaching
troop train

to Kirkpatrick and the north

As these diagrams show (the lower 'zoomed in' on the key area), Quintinshill was caused by a succession of errors and unfortunate timing, with tragic consequences.

It was not the only time Allied troops were run over by trains in Britain. On 24 September 1917 ten soldiers from the New Zealand Expeditionary Force were killed at Bere Ferrers, Devon. Told that they would receive food at their first stop at Exeter, when their train made an unscheduled stop at Bere Ferrers many left the train, mistaking their location for Exeter. Some jumped from the train on to the Plymouth-bound tracks where they were hit by a London Waterloo to Plymouth express. Nine died instantly and another later in nearby Tavistock Hospital.

and made their way across the tracks to what they thought was safety.

The safety was an illusion: Wallace remembered the next express and shouted a warning to the troops to get out of the way. It was too late. As the 0605 express approached Quintinshill, the driver, Andrew Johnstone, saw a guard waving his arms – a recognised and universal railway action that in a last resort instructs a train to stop. 'I immediately shut off steam and set my brake to zero, and attempted to reverse the engine, but before the last could be done my train collided with the wreckage,' he recalled in the accident investigation.

The express had run over some of the survivors of the troop train and as it hit the wreckage the locomotive overturned, its three leading coaches telescoping into each other and being squeezed, derailed and overturned by the wreckage. It was already a horrific accident – and, now, fire made it even worse. The fires from the steam locomotives added to blazes started by the gas lighting in many of the carriages, creating an inferno it was impossible for rescuers to approach. Explosions from the gas cylinders which supplied lighting to many of the coaches created an extra, unwelcome danger. With no local water supply the fire spread rapidly, burning out all bar six vehicles of the troop train and the four leading coaches of the express. Nothing could be done for the wounded in the carriages: 227 troops, passengers and railway staff – including the driver and fireman of the troop train – died, and a further 246 survived their injuries. It was and still remains the worst ever railway accident in Britain. Among the casualties were four children whose bodies were never identified or claimed. They rest in the Western Necropolis, Glasgow, while the bodies of all of the adults were buried in a mass grave at Rosebank Cemetery, Edinburgh.

Blame was placed squarely on Meakin and Tinsley – who received eighteen months' imprisonment and three years' penal servitude respectively. Hutchinson, despite not following the safety rules to the letter, was found not guilty of culpable homicide and breach of duty. That Meakin and Tinsley had made a vast error is undoubted – the railway has strict rules of operation and if they had adhered to them the accident would not have happened. And those pressures of 'total war'? Britain's railways *were* under pressure, but the widely held view of the time was that Quintinshill was no busier than it might have been on a bank holiday. Few if any blamed the addition of an extra empty coal train and a troop train (which in peacetime might easily have been an excursion train or a relief for a busy express, and goods trains often ran late) for the disaster.

The Royal Scots were due to embark from Liverpool for Gallipoli but all of the enlisted men and one who survived were restricted to home duties for a short period. They had suffered trauma on a par with anything they could have experienced at the front line: it was a compassionate and just decision on the part of the military authorities, so often unfairly maligned for their harshness towards the troops under their command.

Big changes were afoot near Quintinshill, too. A massive new ammunition factory was being planned at Gretna, claimed to be the biggest in the world. Nine miles long and two miles wide, it would stretch from Eastriggs in the west, past Gretna and across the border to Longtown, near Carlisle. Chosen for its good rail connections and relative remoteness, it would produce 1,000 tons of cordite every week, employing 20,000 workers (mostly women), and have an internal railway system running over 125 miles of tracks and requiring 34 locomotives to operate. Getting the products of factories like Gretna to the front lines was a different matter, however. With millions of soldiers to support on either side of the lines, supplying them would pose a massive headache for the Allies and Central Powers alike.

5

FEEDING THE
FRONT

FEEDING THE FRONT

1915 saw the war of mobility on the Western Front end. The Allies and the Central Powers now had to reinforce and supply their growing armies – and evacuate the wounded in a growing trial of strength.

Few generals (with the notable exceptions of Britain's Kitchener and William Robertson) expected the Great War to become a long-term trial of strength, but in 1915 it became clear that the demands of trench warfare vastly exceeded those of a short mobile conflict. With poor roads and motor transport in its infancy it was inevitable that the rail networks of France and Belgium would play the main role in supplying the needs of the front line, and the strengths and weaknesses of railways very quickly became clear.

To prepare for a major offensive – and with Germany content to rest on the defensive, for the moment the onus was on the Allies to attack – meant delivering troops, ammunition, horses and supplies to the fighting area, and the French *gare régulatrice* system was by far the best way of doing this. Even with all the pre-war planning, though, the existing railway facilities at places such as Amiens were too small to cope with the unprecedented demands of the armies in the field. With the British and Commonwealth contribution growing rapidly, too, France's rail network was already being strained in early 1915, and the demands were set to grow.

On both sides of the front line military traffic took priority over everything else and a massive planning effort was undertaken to ensure that the needs of the front could be met. This probably affected the Germans more than the Allies. Whereas the French rail network was largely intact and worked by staff familiar with it, Germany had to repair Belgium's shattered network and then assess how best to use it.

Neither did it have access to much of Belgium's rolling stock, so it had to fall back on plans to use German equipment instead. Germany's railway managers almost worked miracles in being able to run a military train every twenty minutes twenty-four hours a day on parts of the Belgian network by early 1915. To achieve so much in such a short space of time was yet another brilliant piece of German railway operation.

Across the board there was now a real recognition that to get the forces in place to secure a victory depended on intense but realistic railway operation. Slots in the timetable were allocated to military trains whether they ran or not and civilian traffic took

second place if it ran at all. The capacity was there for the Germans to run trains every twenty minutes, but it was operational requirements from the front line which dictated whether they did or not.

The big problem with using railways to supply a front line is that it is very difficult to conceal intentions. Soldiers can be billeted in civilian buildings, and artillery and ammunition concealed, but it is impossible to hide a large marshalling yard for wagons and troop trains, and equally so to disguise the much needed expansion of railway facilities to support a major offensive from reconnaissance aircraft flying over the support and rear areas where the main railheads were. German air reconnaissance had vastly improved from late 1914 to early in 1915 with the introduction of Albatros two-seater types with greater ranges. Also, from the off the German army had their own observation balloons whereas the BEF had none of their own until spring 1915. Worse still, the smoke and steam from the locomotives could be visible from a long way off even on the ground: from the air when build-ups were happening a pilot would be able to see a procession of trains heading to the front, an absolute giveaway that something was happening.

Above: *When trains arrived at railheads they were unloaded on to lorries as seen here – or, equally often, horse-drawn transport.*

Despite these limitations the trains had to run, but while getting troops and supplies to the front line had been well planned by both sides, other matters hadn't. The shifting logistical requirements of the front and facilities such as supply depots, reinforcement camps, training facilities and hospitals added extra pressure and traffic, complicating even the simplest operation. But by far the biggest omission by France and Germany was providing adequate means to take wounded soldiers from the front to recover behind the lines in safety and be conveyed to more distant hospitals across the Channel. Ambulance trains were needed quickly and here Britain's railway companies took the lead.

THE AMBULANCE TRAINS

Early plans envisaged six ambulance trains of thirty-three French goods wagons for the wounded, brake vans for stores and a carriage for the medical staff. The wagons were fitted out with a Bréchot framework to support stretchers and each train could carry 396 wounded soldiers lying down.

There were problems with these trains from the start. The biggest by far was that there was no corridor connecting the wagons, so doctors and nurses had to stay in their wagon until the train stopped and they could swap. That was the theory, but in practice medical staff often took the highly risky decision to climb on to the outside of the wagons and cross the gap between the buffers and enter the next one while the train was on the move.

The first real attempt to improve the situation came from the British Red Cross, which wanted to have its own trains in France. It made a private arrangement with the Wagon-Lits Company to create

Left: Railways supplied forces in every theatre. Field railways were used in Asia Minor as well as Europe, and in April 1917 a combination of Turkish and German troops prepare to unload a narrow-gauge train at Jarischaschi in Asia Minor. The locomotive driver is wearing German uniform.

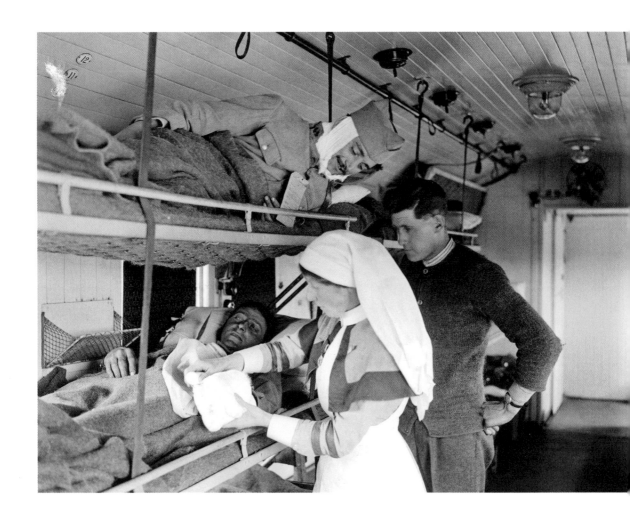

Above: Nurses dress wounds of French and British soldiers in an RAMC ambulance train near Doullens on 27 April 1918. Two nurses tended seriously wounded patients, another walking wounded, and there was one for officers, who was also the sister in charge.

Right: The Germans used metre gauge railways where they were captured in Belgium, and this image shows the mixture of trains, automotive transport and horses used to keep supplies flowing.

a train formed of sleeping cars (which were obviously more suitable for wounded patients and which had corridor connections at the ends), dining cars and normal passenger coach, manned by Red Cross staff. Its capacity was far less than the French ambulance trains but much more suitable for medical needs. It was soon split up and the vehicles used in other ambulance trains, but the point had been proved superbly.

Attention now turned to Britain, whose domestic ambulance trains were vastly superior to anything running in Europe. The first, converted largely from brake vans and with connecting corridors and continuous brakes, which prevented the jolting for which he early French trains were notorious, arrived in France with seven in use by 17 September 1914, and from then on a steady stream of British ambulance trains were sent to France. Their capacity compared well with the early and unsuitable French trains, carrying 306 lying down cases and up to sixty-four sitting cases.

The British Red Cross again came to the fore and a donation of £24,000 by the United Kingdom Flour Millers' Association paid for the construction of two by the Great Western and Great Eastern railways. They were built to War Office specifications and arrived in France in spring 1915. Once overseas they were funded jointly by the army, the Friends' Ambulance Unit and the Joint War Committee. They were crewed entirely by Red Cross personnel except for a Royal Army Medical Corps (RAMC) officer who commanded the train, and from the end of 1915 by Friends' Ambulance Unit orderlies. It was then decided that a number of standard trains should be built by various British railway companies to War Office specifications and altogether thirty were eventually sent to the military forces overseas, mostly in France and Flanders.

These standard British ambulance trains were sixteen coaches long, and in addition to the accommo-

dation for the wounded included a pharmacy coach, two kitchens, a mess coach for the staff and a brake and stores van.

Wounded soldiers weren't, of course, taken straight from the front lines on to an ambulance train: they couldn't be right at the front in any case, and operating on casualties, while possible, was best undertaken at a fixed facility. The first was a Casualty Clearing Station staffed with surgeons and nurses and they compared well with civilian hospitals well behind the lines. Only when cases were stabilised were they taken from there to a base hospital by ambulance train, and, in the case of British wounded, to Southampton on board ship. The port of Boulogne became the main departure point for wounded veterans heading home and its performance was remarkable. Hundreds of casualties could be and were unloaded from the trains in less than an hour (the record seems to be 123 casualties in nineteen minutes). At the main British reception ports of Southampton and later Dover, a ship of 200 stretcher cases and 300 walking wounded could be unloaded and patients transferred to domestic ambulance trains in less than two hours to one of 196 receiving stations all over the country – usually as near to their homes as possible – for onward road transport to hospital. By any measure, the consideration given to the wounded was one of the few bright spots in this conflict.

Whether operated by the Red Cross or the RAMC, the routine on an ambulance train was largely the same. Once the patients were settled the nurses assessed each man and his diet and then, after receiving treatment instructions from the medical officers, set down to their work.

Right: Wounded soldiers weren't simply loaded on to trains at the front line. Following initial treatment they were taken by road to a railhead where they were gently loaded on to ambulance trains for onward transport, in this case to Boulogne-sur-Mer (Pas-de-Calais) in 1915.

The work was hard, with nurses and medical officers working non-stop to care for their patients. Twenty-hour journeys were not unknown when the rail network was highly congested, and on most trains there was a constant procession of patients heading to the treatment room to have their dressings changed. This could easily amount to 300 dressings, and on long journeys many would have to be changed twice if not more.

There was opposition early in the war to nurses serving on ambulance trains at all, something Nurse Mary Stewart-Richardson found on one of the French trains in September 1914:

> I found a very decided spirit of opposition to our boarding the train at all. For the Officer Commanding (whom later, I held in the highest respect & esteem, for his many excellent qualities and able management) was to say the least of it, not encouraging, and vowed there was no accommodation for us, no means of feeding us, and altogether not only would we be greatly in the way, but he considered we were wholly unnecessary as a portion of the train staff.
>
> I told him firmly that my orders were to proceed on the train with the other three Sisters, and those orders I intended to carry out. Further that we were there to be of as much use, and to give as little trouble as possible, and that those were also our firm intentions. He looked at me speechless and then climbed into a First Class compartment into which I quickly followed him, with the other Sisters, making up my mind that once I had set foot in that train, not to leave it again.

Later in the war the efforts and dedication of the nurses and orderlies were widely recognised, but in the early stages they most definitely were not. The Red Cross's role wasn't just in funding and staffing ambulance trains. One of its most important roles was the provision of Rest Stations to act as dressing stations and provide hot food and care for patients travelling from the front to base hospitals.

In the British Red Cross's official history of its activities in the Great War, Dame Katherine Furse, who took two members of the Voluntary Aid Detachment (VAD), an organisation set up by the Red Cross and Order of St John, recalled the spectacle at the first Rest Station in Boulogne:

> On November 2 I went down to the Rest Station at about 10am and found the trucks almost empty and was told that the Staff were feeding a train at the other side. Going over, I found the VADs giving soup or cocoa to an immense number of wounded men, mainly walking cases. These men were haggard and dirty; their wounds were streaming with blood, their dressings soaked through as practically nothing had been done for them since they left the Dressing Stations. They had come down in an empty supply train which had wandered unexpectedly into Boulogne and they had a further journey of about 15 hours on to Rouen … I told the Medical Officer of the train that we had three trained nurses and plenty of material and could change or pack the dressings for the men if he liked. He accepted gratefully, gave an order and almost before one could look round, a queue of wounded men was waiting outside our dispensary … We worked for hours and several cases, being very severe, were picked out and sent to Hospital on our authority.

THE BRITISH INFLUENCE GROWS

France had benefited from the relocation of 1,850 Belgian locomotives and 9,000 carriages and wagons evacuated during the German invasion but, despite this very welcome addition to the nation's resources,

Right: British soldiers take cover in a French goods brake van at Beaucourt-Hamel on 13 November 1916 after the capture of the village on that day by British troops. Only one wall and this van remained of the station.

Above: The devastation in the front lines was massive. This was once Guillemont station, but by September 1916 barely a trace remained after its capture by Allied troops. Shells are still bursting in the background.

towards the end of 1915 the rail network of northern France in particular was approaching breaking point. Although the British were planning for a breakthrough and the likelihood that her armies would eventually need to use and possibly operate the railways in Belgium, while the front line was in France the expectation was that the French railway network would supply both countries' forces.

In January 1915 the British decided to create a railway section in the army with a view to the expected Belgian operations. Three of the 270-strong sections were dedicated to maintaining locomotives and two to operating the railways. The Midland Railway's highly regarded Superintendent Cecil Paget was placed in charge of the new Railway Operating Division. He was given a temporary commission as major and placed in charge of railway operations in Europe.

The first railway soldiers arrived in France in summer 1915 and their initial task was to take over shunting operations in Boulogne docks and prepare supply trains for onward transport by French railways. It was a small move but it helped relieve the pressure on France at a port which dealt almost exclusively with British needs. A small detachment was charged with learning the twenty-one-mile-long Hazebrouck to Ypres railway, which was operated by the French following the inevitable problems caused by Germany's near takeover of Belgium. The Railway Operating Devision began operating the route from 1 November 1915. Work was also undertaken to double this single-track railway as when the British marched into Belgium it was widely expected to be one of the key transport arteries.

This relatively small project, which started in June 1915, was just one of many expansions and enhancements of the railway networks behind both sets of front lines that were needed to keep the armies supplied. All along the Western Front in France and Belgium engineers beavered away to connect supply dumps to the rail network, expand sidings and install the water supplies for locomotives, signalling systems and all of the other needs of the railway. All of this had to be based around the existing rail networks of France, Germany and Belgium: broadly speaking, all of the combatants had to work with the key routes they had in 1914, and any additions to the railway had to be very carefully considered in order not to add too much traffic to heavily used routes and create operating bottlenecks with their inevitable delays.

With France firmly in charge on the Western Front, this meant that when the British wanted a new connection to, say, an ammunition dump, it had to ask the French for permission. Only after a comprehensive assessment of the impact on existing operations would permission be granted, and from 1915 onwards, usually with the proviso that the British supplied the labour and materials needed. Ammunition dumps were particularly sensitive and they were located where double handling of bullets, shells and explosives could be minimised. The rule with live ammunition is simple: the less it has to be handled, the less chance there is of something going badly wrong.

GOING OFF THE RAILS

The Allies faced two major problems with their railways in 1915. The first was one of manpower, and in the crisis of 1914 all but the most essential railway staff were called up to the army. If the war had lasted the six months or so widely predicted this wouldn't have been a major problem but as it dragged on through 1915 the manpower shortage became increasingly acute. Retirement was delayed for older employees, which helped, but with few young men joining the railways keeping the trains serviceable in the first place became ever more difficult. Shortage of maintenance staff and spare parts as French industry was directed to munitions production meant that locomotives, carriages and wagons were running far beyond the time when they would normally have been overhauled. Reliability was being eroded continuously and as rolling stock broke down the repairs backlog grew and grew. It was as well that artillery shells were in short supply in 1915 because if it hadn't have been there was every chance that the railways couldn't have got them to the front in time.

The shell shortage of 1915 also led to the rail network becoming congested with short trains carrying whatever was available. This went against long-established principles of rail operation that state that when it comes to goods trains the ideal is to run relatively few long trains to a destination rather than dozens of shorter ones. These short trains were eroding scarce track capacity, but the need to move supplies and soldiers as quickly as possible meant that in 1915 the niceties of civilian railway operation were disregarded for the sake of operational requirements.

British and Commonwealth troops were starting to arrive in France in considerable numbers and this placed yet more strain on the network. The BEF grew from six divisions of British regular army and reserves in 1914, by another six new divisions by the end of 1914 and by March 1915, the number had increased to twenty-nine. The 3rd Army was formed in July 1915 and with the influx of troops from Kitchener's volunteers and further reorganisation, the 4th Army in 1916. To put this in context, a division in 1914 normally consisted of around 18,000 men and although it varied as the war went on there were normally about two or more divisions to a corps and two or more corps to an army.

When the first Indian Corps arrived in France after a lengthy sea journey they landed at Marseilles and were taken from there to the front via Orléans. These journeys were long and arduous for soldiers and railwaymen alike, but bit by bit the Allied armies were massing. The British still expected to be able to break through the German lines and pursue the war of manoeuvre they believed would be decisive; the French wanted to regain their lost territory. In truth, though, there was neither the men, infrastructure nor expertise on either side needed to win outright in a new and evolving form of warfare.

British offensives at Neuve Chapelle in March 1915 and Loos in September and October, as well as French attacks in Artois in February, June and September saw huge losses suffered for little territorial gain. Germany's only major offensive on the Western Front that year at Ypres, in Belgium, reduced a salient by around two-thirds but again both sides suffered heavily without decisive result.

It was clear that more of everything – men, horses, ammunition, railways and rolling stock – was essential to gain victory. Many years later, United States Marine Corps General Robert H. Barrow said: 'Amateurs think about tactics, but professionals think about logistics.' In 1915 the best tactics of the time had failed in the face of machine-gun and artillery fire. In the absence of a breakthrough British and French generals now realised they had to pay much more attention to their armies' 'tails'. The British finally embraced the need for railway operation to become a key part of the army's operations, and the following year, 1916, would see the Railway Operating Division play an ever-increasing role.

Left: During the German advance of March–July 1918 supply trains sometimes found themselves on the wrong side of the lines. The German soldiers look happy having acquired liquid refreshment: the British soldier is likely to be a newly captured prisoner.

THE NEEDS OF THE FRONT

It wasn't just keeping troops and horses fed, watered and supplied with ammunition that occupied the railways: an enormous and admirable effort went into providing some of the comforts of home at the front line. Mail was perhaps the most important traffic – a hugely difficult organisational task but one that the Post Office largely succeeded in. Newspapers from home were important, too, with around 20,000 a day delivered to the largest British formations. Fifteen wagonloads of plum puddings were delivered for Christmas 1915; materials for the YMCA establishments near the front line were carried, too, along with much else that on the face of it was far removed from fighting needs.

Among the more unusual and today treasured cargoes was the 'Princess Mary' tin. Following national newspaper advertisements seeking donations to the Sailors & Soldiers Christmas Fund – an organisation created by King George V's seventeen-year-old daughter Princess Mary – almost every soldier serving at the front and every sailor afloat received an embossed brass box containing items including tobacco, cigarettes and a pipe for smokers (non-smokers received a packet of acid tablets, writing case, paper and pencil), and, depending on their location and role, other gifts which might include chocolate for nurses, spices for Indian troops, and for those not serving afloat or on the front line a bullet pencil. The boxes contained a Christmas card and picture of the princess, and prisoners of war had theirs reserved until they came home.

On the way back, in addition to mail other cargoes were rather more poignant: trains heading back from the front carried the personal effects of the deceased. Trains carried empty petrol tins, damaged equipment, sick horses, prisoners of war, broken-down road vehicles and much else.

VALENCIENNES.

THE SOMME AMBULANCE TRAIN FIASCO

Sir Henry Rawlinson, General Officer Commanding 4th Army, had taken great pains to ensure that no breakdown in the evacuation of casualties was likely to reoccur during the impending offensive, as had happened the previous year during the Loos attacks. He estimated that twelve ambulance trains and six temporary ambulance trains would be required daily to cope with the expected 10,000 casualties per day. This was intended to include enough capacity to avoid undue crowding and discomfort for the wounded. The temporary ambulance trains were assembled to transport large numbers of lightly wounded men and each could carry up to 1,000 sitting patients.

On the first day of the battle, 1 July, the medical units were being stretched by mid-morning. Casualty Clearing Stations (CCS) were rapidly filling but as yet there was no particular concern as the ambulance trains had been allotted and were expected to be called forward imminently to evacuate the wounded.

By midday, with the medical services working flat out at the CCSs, it was becoming clear that the non-arrival of enough ambulance trains meant that something had gone badly wrong: only one train had arrived. A previous train had left for the base hospitals at Rouen with a load of 487 patients, but more than half of these were sick and most of the remainder wounded from the 30 June.

As the day wore on, the CCSs called for twelve of the eighteen ambulance trains but, inexplicably, only three trains had been standing by in the 4th Army area. In addition to the solitary train that had arrived in the morning, just two more turned up that afternoon. Urgent messages were sent out to other British Army units but by the end of the day only another two had arrived, making a total of five for the day. The conditions at the CCSs, already chaotic, deteriorated appallingly. Casualties placed in the open because of lack of space inside had to spend the night there in pain and often with untreated wounds, hoping that it would not rain or that German shells would miss them. Motor ambulances arriving with further wounded from the front were turned away by CCSs now full to capacity and sent elsewhere. At least 32,000 were wounded on the first day in 4th Army, whose CCSs had adequate accommodation for only 9,500 cases.

What had happened to the missing ambulance trains? For the next three days after 1 July concerted efforts were made to get the wounded away from the front and every available train within the BEF remit was worked around the clock. In total during this period ambulance trains made fifty-eight journeys from the front carrying 31,214 wounded from the 4th Army zone – evidence of what might have been achieved on the first day when five trains had transported fewer than 4,000 casualties. By contrast, 4,000 men wounded from the 3rd Army's diversionary attack to the north of the main thrust of the attack were all treated and processed with the minimum of delay and sent on their way.

In July 1916, 118,496 casualties arrived at Dover and Southampton. From 3 to 9 July, more than 47,000 reached these two ports. In the middle of that week – 6 July – a record 10,112 were landed, 7,902 at Southampton and 2,210 at Dover. These figures would not be matched for the remainder of the war. That day twenty-nine trains were despatched from Southampton and eight from Dover to various destinations. Some of these trains performed two journeys, often stopping en route to remove serious cases to the nearest hospital.

No satisfactory explanation of the lack of ambulance trains on that first day of the Somme was ever made public. However, the senior officer responsible for the movement of the ambulance trains on 1 July was recalled from active service at the end of 1916 and retired – evidence if nothing else that, despite being in a painful learning curve, the army was prepared to act decisively to look after its wounded.

In Eastern Europe, where by 1915 German armies were already on Russian territory, having beaten the initial attack, railways had a rather different impact on the war in this sparsely populated and underdeveloped region. On the Eastern Front, the railways were much more involved in the actual fighting ...

'Il a été mangé par la Gare de l'Est' – *'Eaten by the East Station'*

Attributed to French mothers in Paris wondering where their sons had gone.

Previous page: Valenciennes was held by German forces for most of the war. After its recapture by the Allies in 1918, Allied servicemen contemplate the devastation of the town's railway station.

Above: Prisoners of war were put to work by all sides, and, to compensate for their menfolk serving at the front, French railways used POWs for menial tasks such as cleaning the stations.

6

WAR IN
THE EAST

WAR IN THE EAST

Russia's speedy mobilisation caught Germany by surprise thanks to effective use of its railways. On the Eastern Front railways – and the lack of them – meant the war was very different from that in the west.

From the moment war was declared it was always likely that war between Russia and Germany would be much more prolonged than that in the west. The Germans had recognised this from the start by seeking to defeat France quickly and then turn its attention east to Russia, but the speed of Russia's mobilisation was impressive: its invasion of Germany was to take place on 17 August – weeks before the Germans expected.

Except around major cities Russia's rail network was sparse but some key strategic links existed, and some of those linked the borders of Austria-Hungary and eastern Prussia east of Warsaw in a way that – in theory – allowed Russia to switch troops from either of its expected enemies.

Furthermore, 40 per cent of the army was in the west in peacetime, which was probably the key factor in Russia's ability to mobilise its troops faster than Germany was prepared for. There were 744 battalions of infantry and 621 of cavalry to be moved, with 544 and 361 respectively reaching detraining points on day eighteen, and eleven days later the overwhelming majority of the initial forces were

ready for action in the terms understood by the Russians at the time.

The big issue in Poland and Ukraine was that the sparsely populated regions of both countries simply didn't require the dense and tightly interlinked rail networks that Germany and France had developed. A conscious decision had been taken *not* to develop the rail network to any great extent in these territories in order to deny an aggressor an easy way into the Russian heartland: memories of Napoleon's advance to Moscow were buried deep in the national consciousness and there was a determination to deny routes of advance to invaders. But infrastructure works both ways: in and of itself it is neutral and can be used for attack or defence; on the offensive a comprehensive railway network allows armies to be sent to the front fresh and rested rather than having to march; on the defence forces can be quickly switched to meet new threats. Unless you completely destroy a railway or

Opposite: The distances on the Eastern Front meant that soldiers spent an awful lot of time on trains. It took a lot of detailed management, and the man in the foreground is busy checking the train's inventory at a wayside stop.

oad on the retreat, the same route used to attack can by definition be used by an invader in return.

With few major population centres and great distances between them, it would have been impossible for Russia to justify the sort of investment Germany had undertaken along the Belgian border. It is expensive to build a railway; once that has been done the tracks have to be maintained (at the time by gangs of workmen walking along them and making repairs where needed), signalling installed and signalboxes manned in order to provide a route with useful capacity and ensure safety, provision for watering, fuelling and maintenance of locomotives and rolling stock provided, and crews employed to man the trains and stations. Even if it had been possible to build a rudimen-

tary rail network along German lines before 1914, the lack of revenue-earning passenger and goods traffic on these long routes would have made them hopelessly unviable. The only way Russia could have justified building such a network was if it was vastly rich, economically sound and utterly terrified of the Germans and Austro-Hungarians. In 1914 it was none of these. At the time, the Russian army, government, press and public opinion were all critical of the railways, and even the Ministry of Ways of Communication, which managed the railway network, fell upon its sword and admitted that the traffic situation was desperate and that new construction prior to 1914 was insufficient for the country's peacetime needs, let alone the long-term demands of a huge war on its borders.

German defence, however, rested on its railways and the investment it had made in strengthening routes in the east. A figure often quoted is that for every yard of Russian track per square mile, Germany had ten. French and German reserves moving forward to the front travelled between 150 and 200 miles whereas the Russian average was more like 800. (A general commanding a Siberian unit observed that he had been on a train for twenty-three days before reaching the front.) Germany knew that the Russians would attack from the south and south-east as extensive fortifications and defence lines in the north and centre acted as a compelling deterrent, but which one it should respond to first was the key question. When Russian troops crossed the border on 17 August from the east, and then from the south five days later, it was able to choose. They attacked the Russian 1st Army's incursion from the east first but then, after tactical setbacks, decided to attack the Russian 2nd Army and withdrew troops from that part of the front line and in one day – 25 August – sent them by rail to the southern border of East Prussia to attach II Army's left flank. The Battle of Tannenberg, fought from 26 to 30 August, saw the Germans stop and then virtually surround the Russians, and this was made possible by Germany's use of the railways to switch troop formations and retain a high degree of flexibility. It offered proof that Germany's railway improvements in the east were as well suited to defence as those in the west were to attack. Again, German planning had worked well within its own borders. A clear and comprehensive railway operation had provided flexibility and there was always the fall-back option of transferring troops back from the west if needed.

It was very different for Austria-Hungary. Set on attacking Galicia – part of present-day Poland and Ukraine – road and rail links were poor to non-existent. Furthermore, Austria-Hungary's army, uniquely among the major combatants, was actually smaller in terms of the troops it could send to fight than it had been almost fifty years before, even though its population had increased massively. Railway links within Austria-Hungary from the populated south to the north-east were poor, meaning that from the outset Austria-Hungary was operating at a massive disadvantage.

Austria was also conflicted between attacking Serbia with a decisive force and conducting a holding operation and focusing on the Russians (by far the greater threat) first. Railway planners were told to prepare to treat parts of the army separately in terms of mobilisation and deployment in a bid to provide flexibility. Even in peacetime this is a near-impossible task: to put it more prosaically, imagine if all the spectators at the FA Cup final were to travel home by train, but with no decision taken until the last minute on whether to travel, for instance, by the Chiltern or West Coast Main Line routes. The result would be chaos, and it was no different for Austria-Hungary when it came to deploying its armies. Twelve divisions were retained as a flexible reserve to be deployed either to Serbia or Galicia but inevitably it would take time for them to reach wherever they were needed – and by the time they got there it might be too late.

There was then an almighty cock-up. On 31 July, with part of the force earmarked for Galicia on its way to the Balkans, when Russian intentions were clear Austrian Chief of Staff Franz Conrad von Hötzendorf tried to turn his southern forces around mid-journey and send them back north. It was theoretically possible but only at the expense of operational chaos and delay, as chief railway experts confirmed. Incredibly these troops travelled all the way to Serbia where they were detrained and then put on troop trains heading north-east. It made good sense operationally and thankfully for Austria-Hungary railway planners had incorporated flexibility into the timetables and deployment plans. More importantly, they had allowed for wide margins of error in the timetables, meaning that although journeys were much longer than they might have been, by accelerating the trains to something approaching normal speeds they were able to catch up.

Austria had at best a naive view of its railway capacity – or at least the military did. When freight trains routinely operated hundred-wagon trains over busy routes the military didn't believe any transport required more than fifty. More trains than were needed had to run, and, worse still, it seemed that they had no concept even of what their railways could do. In *The Eastern Front 1914–1917* Norman Stone cites the example of the Budapest–Przemyśl line, a double-track main line capable of carrying heavy loads: the military believed it was little more than a branch line. Such basic failures of internal intelligence were inexcusable. And by demanding that all trains travelled at the speed of the slowest, irrespective of line speed or motive power, Austria-Hungary's military handicapped itself for a lack of basic information and common sense.

In *The Eastern Front 1914–1917*, Stone wrote: 'III Army Command left Bratislava at 0600 on August 5 and arrived in Sambor at the same hour on August 10 – a performance of which a healthy walker would have been capable.' Austria-Hungary's railway operations in 1914 were lamentable, and its out-of-touch and arrogant military were to blame. Outnumbered to begin with and with troops of varying quality and motivation, its poor use of railways compounded difficulties which would only get worse as the conflict continued.

Right: *Austrian soldiers wait with their wives at a station – probably Vienna – before heading to battle in 1915.*

A WAR OF MOBILITY

Unlike on the Western Front the war in the east was one of manoeuvre, and this was because the territory covered was large and transport links – whether road, rail or waterway – poor. Providing reinforcements to a given location was really a matter of luck: if that location happened to be near a railhead then it was possible to do so quickly; if it was not then the troops had to march and by the time they got to where they were needed the chances were that the fighting would have moved on. This inflexibility when it came to reserves repeatedly caused the Russians to miss opportunities on the attack (and sustain breakthroughs with an effective supply chain) and to suffer defeats when on the defence.

Russia was also hampered by problems conscripting its theoretically vast manpower reserves and by the need to defend against Turkey, too. On the key areas of the Eastern Front its numerical superiority over Germany and Austria-Hungary was often marginal if not, initially, non-existent. The Eastern Front was double the length of that in the west, meaning that even if all the manpower available to Russia could have been mobilised the density of trenches would never have matched that in France and Belgium. And why should it? If territory was regarded as too thinly populated for the building of viable railways, what was the point of devoting massive resources to its defence?

Russia's High Command, Stavka, didn't help. Its armies were structured into independent fronts which controlled their rear areas and had the final say in most matters, military or civil. They effectively controlled the railways in their territory and poor communications between the fronts (as well as considerable infighting and claims of priority) meant that Russia was never able to use its railways as effectively as it should have. Stavka could direct Russia's armies but there was never any guarantee that the generals commanding them would comply with the letter of those instructions.

It was an unwritten rule for both Germany and the Allies that when it came to railway operations the military could make requests but it was experienced railway professionals who made the operational decisions about what was or was not possible. In Russia the army made the calls and its organisational structure was simply inadequate to make good use of its transport links. But if the army made the calls the railway still exerted an influence and could block impossible demands. The frustration with the Russian use of railways wasn't that it was totally incompetent – often it was very good – but that the potential was so seldom realised.

GAUGING PROBLEMS

The Russians expected the Germans to attack them in the spring of 1915 and they did so with dramatic effect. Warsaw was lost and the front pushed beyond East Prussia and into the hinterland of Russia itself. There the attack stalled not far beyond the East Prussian border, facing similar problems to the Russians in supply. They weren't helped either by Russia's deliberate choice of a 5ft rail gauge, as opposed to the German and Western European standard (excluding the Iberian Peninsula) of 4ft 8½ inches. Even where railways existed the Germans couldn't run their own trains immediately. Even to begin to do this one of the rails had to be separated from the sleepers, lifted and repositioned 3½ inches inside to make it standard-gauge. The easy option would have been to install a rail inside the wider Russian tracks for German rolling stock but Russia's choice of gauge deliberately made this difficult. A margin of 3½ inches is simply not enough to fit a rail and fix it to the sleepers. To use Russia's rail network Germany either had to regauge it as it went along or use captured rolling stock. (In fact, Germany's progress was remarkable – by the end of 1916 more than 5,000 miles of track had been regauged, making supply of its armies considerably easier.)

Above: Repairing and regauging tracks was a constant headache for railway troops, and the Germans here have a big job on their hands.

As the Germans advanced in late September 1914 in a chaotic series of actions following the Russian offensive against East Prussia, railway lines came within range of German artillery, rendering already slow journeys for Russian troops dangerous, too. Russia began to fear Germany's formidable ability to reinforce trouble spots quickly by rail. France and Britain seemed awed by Russia's putative manpower reserves and often during the war urged the Russians to attack in the east to relieve pressure in the west. (These reserves did, of course, exist but took time to assemble and employ – a total of 15,500,000 were eventually mustered.)

But after failed winter offensives by both sides in 1914/15, Russia's Grand Duke Nicholas is said to have resisted further attacks on East Prussia: 'We

should simply be exposed to the East Prussian railway network,' he is reputed to have said. Nicholas was right: faced with a well-planned and flexible defensive network any form of attack depended on huge numbers of well-trained and motivated soldiers, good reserves of artillery (which the Russians did not at this stage have, having been let down by foreign suppliers) and an element of surprise. Russia had none of these and to have attacked East Prussia without them would only see her lose more and more troops in the likelihood of stalemate.

Austria-Hungary's near collapse in 1915, prompt-

ed by fears of an Italian invasion, caused Germany to consider how it might reinforce its hitherto ineffective ally and Erich von Falkenhayn, Chief of the German General Staff, started to examine how German troops could be transported by rail south of Cracow if needed. The Germans planned their own offensive in Galicia and in May launched it to great effect.

The Russians blamed greater German resources as the reason for its defeat but Russia's biggest problem again was its inability to handle reserves even where railways existed. Journey times were less of an issue than the utilisation of rolling stock, which was lamentable. Germany's ability to extract maximum capacity from even fairly slow single-track

railways was proved decisively in 1914/15 when they took over Russian railways in what is now eastern Ukraine. On poorly laid, single-track railways it managed to channel 494 troop trains and 98 artillery trains on a network the Russians reckoned could only carry a fraction of the traffic. Part of this disparity was because many Russian railways were single-track. That obviously means that trains can only run in one direction over a single railway at any given moment, with trains in opposite directions passing in loop lines before they are allowed to enter the next track section. The well-trained and experienced Germans had a much better concept of how much traffic a single-track railway could carry, and

used its routes – either domestic or captured – to better effect.

Much of this difference in operating quality was because of the standard of the railway staff. Germany's railway troops were well trained and understood what even a basic railway could do – and what it could not. The 40,000 railway troops with which Russia started the war were often illiterate and even the officers had little training. Expansion of this force to 200,000 added only numbers rather than effectiveness.

The biggest single problem on the Eastern Front in railway terms, however, was the need to supply horses with feed. All the combatants in Europe faced the same issue to a degree – when the railways

Opposite: *The Austrians were amongst the most innovative users of armoured trains, and even in 1915 they were heavily protected and armed, as this example in Galicia proves. The most vulnerable aspect was the tracks they ran on.*

Above: *Destroyed bridges were common on all fronts, but, on the Eastern Front, often getting men and materials to them was a major problem. This bridge was demolished in 1915, possibly by the Russians in retreat.*

Above: Locomotives were placed in the middle of armoured trains to limit their vulnerability, but a well-placed shell would penetrate even the armour of this Austrian train in Russia easily, turning it into a static target.

stopped, onward movement of supplies was invariably horse- or mule-drawn. If grain for horses is light it is also bulky and supplying them for the Russians took more wagons – around 1,850 per day, it is estimated – than it did to feed troops, which took about 1,100. The tonnage was double what the troops themselves needed, but without the horses to deliver the soldiers' food they would have starved. Half of its railway resources were devoted to supplying horses, compared with around a fifth that the Germans used. The wagons used to supply horses were denied to troop and ammunition movements, and took up scarce track capacity, placing the Russians under a huge handicap even before battle was joined.

But despite all of this Russia *was* investing heavily in its rail network. Most of it was far behind the front lines and not vulnerable to attack, and the Ministry of Transport was second only to the War Ministry in terms of spending, which almost tripled from 400 million roubles in 1915 to 1,100 million a year later. In the three years from 1914 to 1917 it built around 2,500 miles of new railways, doubled about 750 miles and actually gained rolling stock despite losses to Germany with American imported rolling stock entering the fray from 1915.

The wider Russian economy was dependent on the railway network and it proved unable to cope with the twin demands of transporting soldiers and supplies to the front and keeping Russian manufacturing industry supplied. It was further hampered by the fact that ports of entry for *matériel* from its allies were limited to Vladivostok via the Trans-Siberian Railway, Archangel and, belatedly from 1915, Murmansk – all with railway lines huge distances from the front, which hampered using imports as effectively as the Allies could.

THE ARMOURED TRAINS

One of the distinguishing factors of the Eastern Front was the use of armoured trains to support

infantry and cavalry. The concept itself was far from new: as early as 1848 Austro-Hungarian troops had used rudimentary forms of armoured trains to deal with insurrection, and in the American Civil War both Union and Confederate forces built armoured trains to patrol the tracks and engage in combat. By 1914 it was the British who led the way in developing armoured trains, which were used extensively in the Boer War at the turn of the century to transport infantry rapidly and to allow them to fight from the

trains themselves. The future Prime Minister (and in 1914 First Lord of the Admiralty) Winston Churchill was captured when a British armoured train was defeated by Boer General Louis Botha in 1899, which highlighted their fundamental vulnerability. Unlike an infantry or cavalry unit, which most of the time can move freely across terrain, an armoured train is obviously limited to the tracks on which it runs. Take away the track and you turn a mobile armoured train into a small fixed base. In the Boer War they were

Above: German troops crowd the tender of their locomotive during a stop on its journey to the Eastern Front in 1914. They would not travel on the tender as it was both dangerous and prevented the fireman from working.

Above: Vast numbers of Russian prisoners were captured by the Austrians and Germans on the Eastern Front. An Austrian guard keeps an eye on his charges on a lengthy train crossing a bridge which has received a temporary but massive repair in 1914 or 1915.

useful assets but against a well-equipped and trained continental army their vulnerabilities would, the British believed, render them a liability.

The Germans and the French also recognised this, and aside from the handful of improvised armoured trains used in Belgium early in the war, the only major offensive use of trains was as platforms for rail-mounted artillery which ran on to special spurs facing the front lines, fired their ammunition and then evacuated

play a useful combat role.

Drawing on British experience from the Boer War, Russia built four armoured trains to an identical pattern in 1912. A specially armoured steam locomotive was placed in the middle of the trains, with wagons either side carrying machine guns and field pieces, and a control car – effectively a flat wagon – at either end to act as a sacrificial lamb should the train hit a mine or any sort of obstruction. The initial Russian experiences were positive: one train repelled a German attack near Lvov in November 1914 and then later, when the forces were surrounded by the Germans, evacuated corps headquarters.

In 1915 Germany, Austria-Hungary and Russia all developed their armoured trains, and Russia took the lead. Whereas early trains were best described as mobile forts with a mixture of rifle-firing infantry and small-calibre field guns, from 1915 Russia looked more towards naval design, fitting its trains with turreted guns more similar in appearance to a destroyer and lots of machine guns.

But so far all the armoured trains in use on the Eastern Front depended on steam locomotion to power them. There was no question that steam was the most powerful and fastest option for moving armoured trains but not only did the locomotives need frequent watering, coaling and servicing, they were also something of a mobile bomb themselves. A typical steam locomotive of the period had a boiler operating at pressures of 174 pounds per square inch or more, with a fire that at its hottest would melt the copper of the firebox were it not for heat transferring to the water around it. Should the boiler be holed, water – which under pressure boils far above the 100°C at sea level – would flash to steam, expanding massively and potentially causing the entire boiler to explode. If you can destroy the locomotive, even if the rest of the train isn't badly damaged, for a competent attacking force it is now a set of static targets, albeit ones that can fire back.

before counter-battery fire could target them.

In Russia, though, there was a belief that armoured trains *could* play a useful role. The lack of made-up roads in much of the country made railways more valuable and armoured trains offered a mobile and economic way of protecting them from damage. The Russians also had experience from the defence of Port Arthur from the Japanese in the early twentieth century that reinforced their view that they could

THE TRANS-SIBERIAN RAILWAY

In 1891 the Imperial government authorised the first steps towards the construction of Russia's greatest railway, the Trans-Siberian, running from the suburbs of Moscow for almost 5,800 miles to the only Russian port on the Pacific coast at Vladivostok. On 31 May 1892 Tsar Nicholas II set the first stone of Vladivostok station, initiating a project that would take relatively few years to complete but would claim the lives of many of its labourers. Construction started at Vladivostok and Chelyabinsk, a town situated to the east of the Ural Mountains and over 900 miles from Moscow.

Progress was slowed by the climatic extremes of the route and the nature of the terrain. Almost all of the railway was built through sparsely populated areas and lakes, rivers and mountains had to be negotiated, further challenging the labour force, many of whom were exiles forced from their homes in the west or prisoners from the tsarist labour camps. At the height of construction in the late 1890s the railway employed a workforce of some 84–89,000 men.

One of the sternest challenges faced was caused by the exceptional weather of 1897 when snowmelt and heavy rainfall flooded river systems near Lake Baikal causing the destruction of embankments, retaining walls, locomotives and rolling stock. Entire workers' settlements were also obliterated with huge loss of life while over 230 miles of track were damaged.

Until the construction of a bypass route in 1904, prompted by the war with Japan, there was a break in the route at Lake Baikal which forced the introduction of a rail ferry to link the two sections of the route.

Despite these challenges and bureaucratic incompetence, the railway was completed in twelve years and at the time was hailed as one of the wonders of the world. By comparison, however, the Canadian Pacific Railway – 2,097 miles in length and built under similarly challenging conditions – took just four and a half years to complete in 1885.

With the completion of the route, however, it was soon apparent that there were major flaws in its composition that were later exposed by the military. The single-track line was considered one of the main reasons why Russia lost its war with Japan in 1905. In 1908 the Russian Duma voted additional funds to double-track the entire length of the line but by the outbreak of war in 1914 this had not been completed.

From 1914, despite all these drawbacks the line assumed greater importance as an alternative to Archangel for the routing of war *matériel* to the fronts in Eastern Europe. The final stage of the line's Great War history was achieved in October 1916 with the opening of a second 'all-Russian' alternative route from Chita to Khabarovsk and Vladivostok which avoided the need to use the original but strategically vulnerable line that passed through Manchuria via Harbin.

THE MURMANSK RAILWAY

Russia used many of its 2.5 million Austro-Hungarian and 200,000 German prisoners of war to build railways. One project was the 1,448km-long (899 miles) railway from St Petersburg to the ice-free port of Murmansk on the Arctic Sea. Murmansk and the White Sea port of Archangel were both vital ports for the flow of incoming war *matériel* from the Allies and a rail connection linking Murmansk to the south was becoming imperative – especially as Archangel already had its own rail connection to the south via the railway junction at Vologda.

Construction started on the northern part of the line in 1915 but rapidly fell behind schedule due to the lack of labourers until the employment of POWs was taken up. Around 70,000 POWs were eventually used on the line. Despite the efforts of German and several non-belligerent powers to pressure the Russians into improving working conditions and evacuate the most seriously ill POWs, some 25,000 died while working on this massive project. The line was completed a year behind schedule in early 1917.

Austria-Hungary, whose railway operations had been so lamentable in the war, developed a self-propelled armoured rail cruiser based on French pre-war designs which used small petrol engines to propel a lightly built single-carriage train – in practical terms an omnibus on rails. The idea was to reduce the expense of running services on lightly used railways and today it is the norm across Europe. Austria-Hungarian engineers realised that if they could build a self-propelled, petrol-driven armoured train it would be less vulnerable, and because petrol engines are much smaller for a given power output than a steam engine, an effective armoured train could be developed in a single vehicle. A strikingly modern looking vehicle – called a *Motorkanonwagen* – was developed which had a 70mm gun and machine guns. If it resembled a rail-borne tank (though at this point tanks hadn't been developed), that is exactly what it was.

Russia took the concept further after experiments with lightly armoured machine-gun trolleys with its famed Zaamurets rail cruiser. Based on a bogie flat wagon, two 60hp automobile engines powered it to a top speed of 28mph, more than comparable with average speeds of other traffic on most of the routes it operated on. It had two turrets with 57mm Nordenfelt guns which could fire up to sixty rounds per minute.

The armoured trains were used to patrol the tracks, reinforce trouble spots and attack enemy forces where possible. In the absence of tracked vehicles – the only means of covering rough terrain faster than a horse – they were the only way any side could provide short-notice fire support. They were limited, of course, by the tracks they ran on but they were far more useful in the east than they possibly could have been in the west.

Russia's last major offensive of the war, the Brusilov offensive of June 1916, was aimed squarely at Austria-Hungary in Galicia. The Austrians were pressuring Italy – which had declared war on the Allies'

side – and the Germans bleeding the French dry at Verdun in the west. Russia, as had happened before, was asked to draw Central Powers forces away from the Western Front with an attack that ultimately cost Austria-Hungary one million casualties, and Germany to transfer forces from the west to assist. By targeting Galicia with its poor transport links, Brusilov had tacitly acknowledged Russia's own transport limitations and built his forces up over a wide front, heavily dispersed. In two weeks from 4 June, 200,000 prisoners had been captured by the Russians and in the autumn, when it finally ended, 1.4 million casualties had been suffered by Russia and 780,000 by the Central Powers.

It was possibly the Allies' biggest success of the war in terms of territory gained and losses inflicted on the enemy yet it never achieved the breakthrough the Russians sought. Poor transport links and rough terrain bogged down the advance, reflecting the importance of logistics, but, despite this, it did persuade Austria-Hungary to pause its offensive against Italy and for the Germans to take pressure off the French in particular (who feared their ability to fight on, such was the pressure at Verdun). Austria-Hungary's losses were grievous and had a significant effect on its ability to fight on. Russia would manage the two-week-long Kerensky offensive of three armies in July 1917 under a provisional government but events in early 1917 would see enthusiasm for the war wane. Attention now turned to the Middle East, where the railways played a role in a theatre of war as far removed from the mud of the trenches and Europe as it was possible to imagine.

THE TRANS-SIBERIAN RAILWAY

This map highlights the major difficulties of logistics experienced by Russian forces on the Eastern Front when considering the three major ports at Archangel, Murmansk and Vladivostock used for incoming military supplies from the Allies. In addition to the railway mileages given on the map, to these must be added 450 miles from the nearest Japanese port to Vladivostok, and another 1,935 miles from, say, the port of Hull in England to Archangel. Exacerbating the mileage count were the distances required to move supplies from ports in the United States across the Atlantic or the Pacific oceans.

Although the density of lines improved nearer the borders of the Baltic States and the provinces of western Russia, they remained woefully inadequate in keeping the massive numbers of the Russian army fully supplied.

By comparison, the equivalent distances from the Channel ports to the BEF railheads in northern France were small. Calais to Amiens was about seventy miles, Boulogne to Amiens sixty miles and from the same ports to the major BEF base at St Omer even less, at twenty-five and thirty-five miles respectively. The major Russian supply base at Minsk, although situated in western Russia and nearer the front, was still a jaw-dropping 200-mile-plus journey to Brest-Litovsk and from there almost the same distance to Lvov, one of the bitterly contested areas of 1914–15.

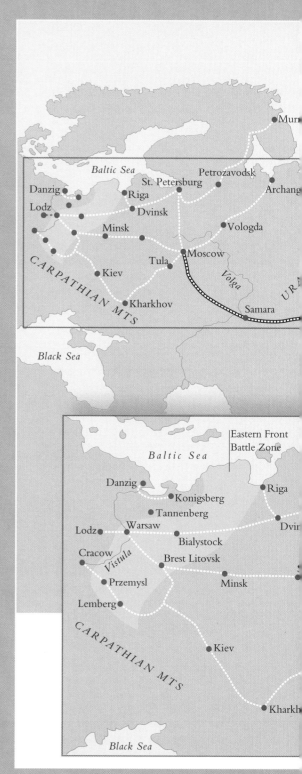

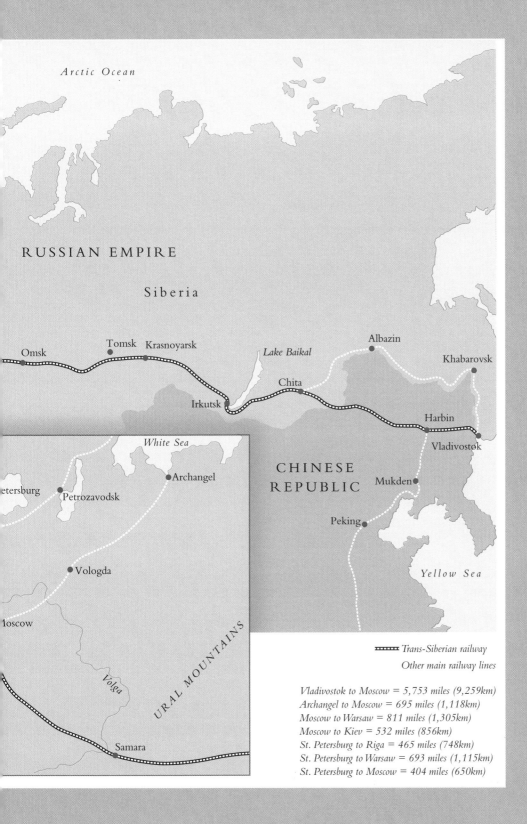

Arctic Ocean

RUSSIAN EMPIRE

Siberia

Omsk Tomsk Krasnoyarsk *Lake Baikal* Albazin Khabarovsk

Irkutsk Chita Harbin Vladivostok

White Sea

...etersburg Archangel

Petrozavodsk

CHINESE
REPUBLIC Mukden

Peking

Vologda

Yellow Sea

...oscow

URAL MOUNTAINS

Volga

Samara

▪▪▪▪▪ *Trans-Siberian railway*
Other main railway lines

Vladivostok to Moscow = 5,753 miles (9,259km)
Archangel to Moscow = 695 miles (1,118km)
Moscow to Warsaw = 811 miles (1,305km)
Moscow to Kiev = 532 miles (856km)
St. Petersburg to Riga = 465 miles (748km)
St. Petersburg to Warsaw = 693 miles (1,115km)
St. Petersburg to Moscow = 404 miles (650km)

7

THE DESERT
RAILWAY WAR

THE DESERT RAILWAY WAR

In the Middle East Britain and the Ottomans faced each other
across the deserts. Rail links were sparse but vital – and the
British had to relearn the lessons so hard won in the Boer War
about supplying its soldiers.

From 1915, when the Ottoman Empire declared war on the Allies, a collision with British
interests in the Middle East was inevitable. The
Ottomans controlled a huge area ranging south from
today's Turkish borders through Syria, Palestine and
into the Arabian Peninsula. The British were dom-
inant in Africa and bordered the Ottomans on the
eastern side of Sinai, Egypt.

British interests were threefold: firstly, Britain
controlled the Suez Canal, the vital artery to India, which obviated the need for ships to make the
lengthy voyage around the Cape of Good Hope;
secondly, it had a major stake in the Persian oil-
fields whose supplies were essential for all manner
of military needs, not least those of the navy, whose
oil-fired Queen Elizabeth Class battleships were
entering service. Finally, its naval bases in the Persian
Gulf allowed it to control shipping through the Strait
of Hormuz and could block any threat to India from
the Middle East. The Ottomans' declaration of war
placed all of these under threat.

The Turks made a concerted attack on the Suez
Canal in 1915 with a 22,000-strong force but the

British repelled it and sought to extend its now
vulnerable defences into the desert. And it was in the
desert that the most demanding railway operations of
the war took place. Turkey's rail network was far from
extensive in 1914, and what had been built had been
funded initially by British and then German interests, but in the Middle East it had completed a major
engineering achievement with obvious strategic
importance – the Hejaz Railway.

Built from 1900 to 1908 and funded largely by
subscription from the Muslim faithful, the purpose
of the Hejaz was to transport pilgrims from the
Ottoman capital Constantinople to the holy cities
of Mecca and Medina, deep in what is now Saudi
Arabia. Before it was built, pilgrims faced forty-day-
long journeys across the desert with all the risks and
hardship that entailed. The new railway cut journey times from Damascus to around five days, an
obvious boon for those pilgrims who could afford
to travel on it. In the event, the railway stopped at
Medina, around 300 miles short of Mecca, but even
so this transformed transport in Arabia. There was
also an obvious strategic benefit for the Ottomans

in being able to supply and reinforce garrisons at Mecca and Medina in particular, and the hope that in time mineral deposits in the region could be extracted by rail.

The Hejaz was built to a gauge of 1,050mm, widely used across the region. The reason for opting for this rather than the standard gauge of 4ft 8½ inches (1,435mm) was that narrower tracks can have tighter curves and the trackbed on which they rest needs less engineering, as do structures such as bridges and tunnels. The trains are smaller and lighter and everything is thus cheaper than a standard-gauge equivalent. Against these benefits are considerations that speeds and loading capacity are rather lower, and that when railways of different gauges coincide passengers and goods have to change trains. But for the Hejaz Railway these weren't major concerns: the comparison wasn't with standard-gauge railways in Turkey or beyond – it was with the alternative land journey.

The sheer challenge of building a railway across a desert is a vast one – construction materials, labour and all the supplies needed to support the engineering have to be brought in. Unlike in Russia or North America, where it was fairly common to source construction materials from nearby forests, the Hejaz Railway could rely on no such benefits. Even today building railways across the desert – as Saudi Arabia is currently doing on a grand scale – is among the most difficult civil engineering projects imaginable: in the early twentieth century such difficulties were

Below: Haidar Pasha railway station (Haydarpaşa Terminal), on the Bosphorus in Istanbul, was one of Turkey's most important railway stations.

even greater.

Operating the railway added yet another layer of difficulty for the Turks. Potential threats from Arab tribes were met by the presence of blockhouses guarding key bridges and tunnels and these needed supplying. (Another frequent problem was theft of wooden sleepers for fuel, resolved in the worst places by the use of iron sleepers instead.) On a steam railway, though, the biggest need – wherever they are – is water for the locomotives. It is fairly easy to provide enough fuel for a day's operation but water is an altogether different matter. Without it the train stops, and if a steam locomotive runs out of water on the move and the train crew cannot remove burning fuel from the firebox in time the boiler explodes. Regular waypoints along the route near water sources were the only way it was possible to operate the railway at all. That it did operate – and well in the normal run of things – is one of the great wonders of the railway world. And while it remained operational the forces it could potentially transport and supply would be a constant threat to British interests.

BRITISH FAILURES

After the Turkish failure to seize the Suez Canal the initiative passed to the British who opted to try to take Baghdad in 1915. With a force of 10,000 men the British advanced from Basra along the River Tigris but suffered a major defeat at the Battle of Kut, losing 1,200 men, and then, after being repelled by a larger Turkish force at Ctesiphon, were besieged at Kut for almost five months before they surrendered. The cause of the British defeat was simple: the initial advance and relief efforts outran their supply lines. There were no railways in southern Mesopotamia and against Turkish forces that could be supplied

Left: The Ma'an Bridge, Jordan, on the Hejaz Railway, was one of the major structures on the route, built to cope with occasional floods. It was a natural target for T.E. Lawrence and the Arabs.

Above: German General August von Mackensen inspects
the Guard of Honour at Sfirkedji station in Constantinople
(Istanbul) on 24 March 1915.

more easily partially if not entirely by the Ottomans'
railways in the region, the British were always facing
a massive challenge.

In 1916 concerted efforts were made in Egypt and
Mesopotamia to address these issues and create a force
which could be sustained in the field and take action
against the Ottomans. From the railhead of Kantara
on the Suez Canal's eastern bank, General Allenby
began to extend the railway across the Sinai. This was
a standard-gauge railway linked to Egypt's system and
fully compatible. By May 1916 the metals reached

Romani in the Sinai and the British push began, the armies this time not overreaching their supplies and advancing, initially at the speed of the railway's construction. By early 1917 the railway had reached the present-day Egyptian border and the Ottoman redoubt of Gaza was finally within reach of a well-trained and -supplied force that could meet the Turks on equal terms. In Mesopotamia the British, too, were building the rail network they had needed in 1915/16, using narrow-gauge (2ft 6inches) tracks with materials from India initially and then metre-gauge (which was also used in the subcontinent) tracks.

The British were now genuinely prepared for the war in the Middle East, but the Hejaz Railway continued to run. If it could be disrupted or, better still, closed, Ottoman garrisons in Mecca and Medina would be cut off, and the Ottoman Empire's ability to reinforce across the region jeopardised. How this happened is one of the most romanticised episodes of the First World War.

THE ARAB REVOLT

When T. E. Lawrence persuaded the generals in Cairo that the Arabs were ready to fight the Turks, the stage was set for one of the few applications of irregular fighting in the Great War. With the Arab Prince Feisal's support the question was how best to fight the Turks. Head-on assaults on Medina were ruled out: as isolated as the garrisons were the Turkish soldiers were well trained and equipped – and in defensive positions. Lawrence and Feisal knew well that such attacks would be suicide.

Their attention focused not initially on defeating Turkish forces in the field but on disrupting them with small-scale actions. The Arabs would attack, inflict casualties and retreat into the desert before the Turks could retaliate in force. The Hejaz Railway, with around two trains a day puffing across the desert carrying soldiers and supplies, was an obvious and vulnerable target. By mirroring tactics used by the Boers against British rail links in South Africa more than a decade earlier, the Turks would be placed on the defensive and forced to respond to keep the railway open.

Lawrence quickly discovered that the quickest and easiest way of disrupting the railway – removing rails – was equally quick for the Turks to repair, and so a 'tulip' mine using 2lb of dynamite was used to buckle the rails beyond reuse. Thus the only way for the Turks to keep the trains running was to laboriously repair the trackbed and install new track. The disruption caused was still relatively minor, however: tracks could usually be repaired in a day or two and services resumed. What Lawrence and the Arabs did, though, was to attack frequently and unexpectedly, detonating the mines under trains if possible.

The locomotive was the obvious target, and when the mine was detonated they were invariably – but not always – damaged beyond repair. Faced with a sudden and immediate halt, carriages and wagons were often derailed and at this point the Arabs poured rifle fire into the carriages as fast as they could. The Turkish soldiers on the trains were never keen on providing target practice for the Arabs and almost always responded quickly, leaving the train and hunting their attackers. Had the Turks caught up with Lawrence and the Arabs in any great numbers they would have surely beaten them.

Lawrence always maintained that the intention of the attacks on the Hejaz Railway was to disrupt rather than close the route. In truth, closing a railway permanently is very, very hard. Tracks can be relaid, bridges temporarily repaired and formations rebuilt – and the Turks did all of these things, repeatedly and tenaciously, and were largely successful in keeping their key supply route to Medina open.

Lawrence's efforts of 1917 grew in strength and were increasingly coordinated with those of General Allenby, whose now well-supplied forces took Beersheba on 31 October after two unsuccessful assaults

Above: *A soldier – claimed to be T.E. Lawrence – inspects*
the wreckage of a train during the Arabian campaign in 1918.

LAWRENCE OF ARABIA – THE MAN BEHIND THE LEGEND

Thomas Edward Lawrence, the second illegitimate son born in 1888 to Irish baronet Sir Thomas Chapman and the family governess, Sarah Maden, later described himself as an 'ordinary man'. But despite such self-deprecation his later exploits in Palestine during the Arab revolt against Turkish rule were to prove anything but ordinary. His parents (who never married) had led a peripatetic existence before finally settling in Oxford after assuming the name of Lawrence.

At Oxford Lawrence developed a strong interest in the Middle East and military history and gained a first-class honours degree in history from Jesus College. As part of his thesis, 'The Military Architecture of the Crusades', he had travelled to Syria in 1909 and in the following years immersed himself in Arab culture, becoming fluent in its language. In 1912 his former tutor, the well-known Arabist D.G. Hogarth, led the British Museum's 1912 archaeological dig at Karkemish in Asia Minor and Lawrence was invited to become part of the team. In 1913 his expertise was again utilised by Hogarth and the archaeologist Sir Leonard Woolley as part of a British Military Intelligence survey mission in the Sinai Desert.

Lawrence was in England when war was declared and, though keen to enlist, was persuaded by Woolley to curb his enthusiasm in favour of attaining a lieutenant's commission in October 1914. His experience of the Middle East and his Arabic language skills were soon recognised by the authorities and he was able to bypass the usual requirements of formal training and was sent to Cairo as part of the Military Intelligence unit. Further trust in his abilities was shown in 1916 when he was tasked by the Chief of the Imperial General Staff William Robertson, to attempt to bribe a Mesopotamian Arab leader with up to £1,000,000 to aid General Townshend's besieged army in Kut.

In June 1916 Lawrence was only twenty-eight and still very junior but was already something of a personality in Egypt. This was partly due to his continued close relationship with Hogarth, who exerted considerable influence within the Arab Bureau in Cairo, but also due to his carefree attitude and general disregard for military etiquette.

In June 1916, the British government entered into an alliance with Arab nationalists who sought to free themselves from Ottoman rule. As part of British efforts to bolster the Arab cause, in October 1916 Lawrence was sent to Arabia as a liaison officer. He met King Hussein's sons, Emir Feisal and Abdullah, and convinced them to coordinate their actions with the wider British strategy in the region. He also dissuaded them from attacking Medina in favour of a guerrilla war against the Hejaz Railway which would tie down considerable numbers of Turkish troops. Now working in full Arab garb Lawrence worked with Feisal to promote a coordinated revolt of the tribes with full British backing in arms and cash.

Lawrence was involved in many actions and was wounded several times and captured once. With Lawrence, Arab forces took the Red Sea port of Aqaba from the Turks in July 1917 and were able to distract considerable numbers of Turkish troops with their hit and run raids while British forces began their invasion of Palestine.

At the end of the war Lawrence's achievements and hopes for an Arab homeland in Syria were undermined by the Sykes–Picot Agreement which divided the Arab provinces of the Ottoman Empire into areas of future British and French control or influence. He died in Britain in May 1935 in a motorcycle accident near Wareham in Dorset.

Below: The war in East Africa saw ambulance trains similar to those on the Western Front used by the British, and, following an action in a long-running campaign, wounded soldiers are lifted aboard.

Opposite: The Hejaz Railway was one of the world's railway masterpieces, and stations such as Ma'an, Jordan, were needed to water the locomotives as well as provide a service. The station may be small, but it has a full set of facilities for passengers and freight.

on Gaza in March and April that year. The Battle of Junction Station on 1–7 November cut Turkey's rail link to Jerusalem and although former Chief of the German General Staff Erich von Falkenhayn helped the Turks to establish a formidable line of defence, British and Commonwealth troops marched into the Holy City on 11 December.

In Mesopotamia, bolstered by much improved rail links, the British recaptured Kut in February 1917 and then Baghdad in March. By November 1917, Tikrit had fallen to the British, too. Troop withdrawals from Palestine and Mesopotamia in 1918 to bolster the Allied effort on the Western Front delayed further action but the stage was set for a decision in the Middle East.

By comparison with other theatres, the forces involved in the Middle East were small but once again the strengths and limitations of the railways played a critical role. The British had apparently forgotten their experience in the Boer War and neglected their supply horribly in Mesopotamia with results that could easily have been foreseen at the time. Equally, Turkey's use of a quite limited rail network in the region probably allowed it to continue opposing the British for much longer than it otherwise would have. Keeping the Hejaz open to supply the garrison at Medina in the face of continued disruption was a tremendous piece of railway operation. It is tempting to ask whether a withdrawal to Palestine might have benefited the Turks in purely military terms, but such an action may well have increased internal conflicts within the region and the Ottoman Empire at large.

Railways had been important in the Middle East and were ultimately used effectively. But in 1917 the Western Front was the focus of the war, and here railway operations had evolved to a fine pitch indeed.

RAILWAYS IN AFRICA

In 1914 Germany's empire included four colonies in Africa – German East Africa (today's Tanzania),

German South West Africa (Namibia and part of Botswana), Cameroon, and Togoland (today Togo and part of Ghana) – and the British sought to evict its imperial rival.

Togoland was taken as early as 26 August 1914 in a joint British–French invasion but the other colonies took rather longer thanks to their greater size, the distances involved for the soldiers, and, in the case of German East Africa, spirited and determined resistance.

The German colonies were effectively marooned by the outbreak of the war, and reinforcement was only possible by sea. South West Africa fell in 1915 and Cameroon in 1916, but German East Africa was an altogether different proposition. The British could and did use the railways of South Africa, Rhodesia and British East Africa in a bid to get forces somewhere near the action, but, as with Arabia, rail links were sparse and not extensive enough to be relied on. The Germans had built some metre-gauge railways and one was built as a route from Tanga, approaching the border with British East Africa at Moshi. A more successful venture was the railway from Dar-es-Salaam to Kigoma on Lake Tanganyika, which opened in 1914.

The Allies built a metre-gauge railway from the railhead at Voi to Maktau and later extended it to Moshi as offensives gathered pace. The Germans were forced to improvise and with such vast territory the limited rail networks were of little use. The Allies had captured both by September 1916, but it wouldn't be until the Armistice in November 1918 that Germany's remarkable resistance in Africa ceased. Allied casualties in a campaign which lasted for the duration of the war were estimated at 100,000, and 160,000 troops who might otherwise have been deployed elsewhere were tied down for the duration had it not been for the German resistance.

Above: In January 1916 a British shooting party rides a train in German South West Africa. The wagon in front wasn't just for visibility: it was to protect the locomotive from obstructions on the tracks.

Next page: The British built a new railway across the Sinai to support its offensive into Palestine, and the supply trains which ran along it were lengthy affairs, as this rare picture of a formation passing El Kirbah on its way to El Arish shows.

8

THE SMALL
RAILWAYS

THE SMALL RAILWAYS

The year 1916 had seen huge battles that stretched transport to the limit. From 1917 the Allies had learned their lessons well and the role of the field railways was expanding rapidly to deal with the insatiable demands of the front lines almost everywhere.

It is a long way from the slate quarries of North Wales to France but a Welsh invention provided the final piece in the railway jigsaw to get soldiers and supplies to the front line. In 1865 the Ffestiniog Railway opened in order to move slate from Blaenau Ffestiniog to the small harbour of Porthmadog. It was built to a gauge of 1ft 11½ inches and was the first major narrow-gauge railway in the world. With rails less than half the width of standard-gauge tracks, the advantages of the later Hejaz Railway in terms of cheaper construction and operation were amplified. Industry in Britain, France and Germany was quick to realise the benefits. A host of companies offered a range of 'standard' designs, some of which still operate today on heritage railways. Tracks could be laid quickly and easily by a handful of men over rough and even unprepared ground, and, in agriculture and quarrying in particular, removed and relaid elsewhere as required.

German and French industry rapidly developed their own mass-produced equivalents and these little railways became common across Europe for industrial use. In South West Africa the Germans experimented with 600mm-gauge railways militarily and found that these little railways were able to keep pace with its armies' advance. Its generals were quick to recognise that similar considerations might apply in a European war and began stockpiling track materials, locomotives and wagons in anticipation of just such a use.

In France the farmer and engineer Paul Decauville's own experiments proved that lightly constructed railways enabled greater loads to be carried from his fields without causing as much damage to the ground as horse-drawn carts; he rapidly developed a sectional system of track with light rails fastened to steel sleepers that could be laid on roads, paths or even open country if drainage was good. Like its counterpart across the Rhine, the French army had been quick to realise their strategic potential in wartime and had also laid down substantial quantities of stocks of this material.

Whether working to the French or German systems the principles were identical. Unskilled labourers or soldiers could quickly assemble prefabricated 5m long sections of track enabling short trains to operate with wagons able to carry around eight tons – almost the capacity of three average-sized road lorries at the time. It would be tempting to describe these railways as being little more than train sets but such a term belies the flexibility and carrying capacity of a 60cm-gauge railway. They may have been smaller than standard-gauge railways but they were a well-conceived and developed concept whose worth had been proven in industry long before the military grasped their potential.

Although Britain pioneered narrow-gauge railways in 1914 it regarded them as already being outdated for military use. Rapid developments in the internal combustion engine and road transport encouraged a British decision to rely on lorries and automobiles to provide transport for its armies beyond the standard-gauge railheads. The British ambitions were at least a generation ahead of automotive technology here. Lorries of the era were unreliable, slow and of poor carrying capacity. Furthermore, they were solid-tyred and on the largely unmade roads of France and Belgium this, combined with their weight, wrecked the road infrastructure more quickly than had been anticipated. In addition, they did not have the capability of travelling across country and over rough ground: beyond the roads the British – to a greater extent than the French and Germans – were utterly reliant on horse and cart and fatigue parties of soldiers to carry loads to the front lines.

Opposite page: *Field railways delivered all manner of things to the front lines – but the most eagerly anticipated were rations, and this little train is carrying sustenance to German troops in 1918.*

SAVING VERDUN

In the event the field railways – to borrow from the German word *Feldbahn* – weren't able to keep up with the German advance in 1914 but once the front had stabilised Germany and France rushed to build and extend their systems. They proved remarkably capable.

Whether French or German, the ability to lay routes quickly and alter them according to operational requirements was a huge asset. They could get much closer to the front line than the standard-gauge routes (six miles was the accepted limit for conventional railways and even at this distance they were vulnerable to long-range shelling) and when they were shelled they were easy to repair and reroute. The German philosophy was generally to build its field railways to something approaching standard-gauge quality with well-built and well-drained trackbeds to carry the loads; that of the French to lay tracks quickly to where they were needed and upgrade them if necessary.

If the British had any doubts about the potential of narrow-gauge railways they were wiped out in 1916 by events at Verdun. Germany's bloody and sustained attack on the French fortress of Verdun from February to August stretched France to the limit, but German assumptions that it would be impossible to supply the front line were wrong. True enough, the standard-gauge railways were cut or were in easy range of artillery fire, but a seventy-five-mile-long metre-gauge railway ran from Bar de Luc paralleling the only usable road to the front lines. Even in France it was never expected that the railway would

Left: Rail-mounted artillery was widely used despite its inflexibility. Germany built two huge guns called 'Big Bertha' to bombard Paris in 1918 from ranges claimed to be as far as eighty-one miles away. The guns were destroyed during the Allied offensive of 1918. Despite the impressive size the guns delivered a poor return for their investment – managing to kill just 620 civilians in the city with their 8.26-inch shells.

be able to supply all the needs, but an hourly service was operated from the start of the German offensive and this was later increased to a train every forty minutes. With a huge effort made to keep the road in good order (almost 9,000 men alone were tasked to do this) the French were able to keep the front line at Verdun supplied with men and shells and the Chemin de Fer Meusien carried around 25 per cent of the materials needed, with a dense network of field railways carrying onwards to the front line. A massive four-month effort also saw a standard-gauge railway built alongside the road by the end of June 1916, enhancing the French logistics capability further.

The Germans had badly underestimated the French and, despite inflicting massive casualties on them, never won the decisive victory here that they expected. The losses incurred by the French at Verdun prompted desperate calls for British and Russian offensives to ease the pressure – which led to the Battle of the Somme in the west and the Brusilov offensive in the east. At a critical time in the war, though, once again France's brilliant railway operation had – just – kept the country in the war.

BRITAIN SEES THE LIGHT

By 1916 the Allied war effort risked a major breakdown due to the stretching of the French transportation network almost to breaking point. It took the muscular and vocal intervention of Eric Geddes (the North Eastern Railway's Deputy General Manager and in 1915/16 Deputy Director General of Munitions Supply) to intervene. He recommended (and, here, a recommendation carried very nearly the weight of an order from the government) that tactical light railway systems should be introduced as quickly and as widespread as possible to avert the growing crisis. Even before Eric Geddes's entry the British military authorities could have responded to the evidence that, in effect, was already lying at their feet. In Belgium a dense network of metre-gauge

lines almost equal in route length to the standard-gauge lines of the country ran along the *pavé* verges, through the streets of towns and villages with an almost profligate ease and disdain for the tight curvatures that would have spelled disaster for any conventional train. In France lines of similar gauge connected villages distant from standard-gauge lines, often ending as remote terminuses to all intents and purposes miles from anywhere. It was June 1915 before the British Army considered the adoption of the metre-gauge standard and the construction of lines of its own connecting to network around Ypres. Matters proceeded slowly and it was September before 50 locomotives and 200 wagons similar to Belgian stock were ordered from home suppliers. It was a start, but metre-gauge railways were too big to operate safely anywhere near the front lines.

As we have seen in Chapter 5, Britain created the Railway Operating Division within the BEF in 1915 and was given increasing responsibility for the operation and maintenance of parts of the French and Belgian railway systems in the British sector. By the end of 1916 the ROD had grown to over 5,000 men with responsibility for 244 locomotives – yet for the soldiers at the front it was the 60cm–gauge field railways that British forces needed and it was the Canadians who led the way, proving in action and on their own initiative that the policies of Germany and France were equally applicable to British needs.

The first Canadian troops arrived in Europe on the Western Front in February 1915 and began to build their own trench tramways using materials either taken over from the French or acquired in their own areas. The logic was sound – a mule or horse could haul much greater loads over even the most lightly laid and improvised tracks than over rough ground alone, and although official British policy was to rely on road transport the Canadians did things their own way, building wagons using a mixture of requisitioned wheels and axleboxes and bespoke bod-

ywork built from whatever materials were to hand. It was helped by the fact that amongst the troops were railwaymen who were well used at home to laying temporary tracks and improvising solutions as they went along. This combination of Canadian experience in the field and Geddes's recommendations finally forced the British Army to accept the need for field railways and to make full use of them.

The British moved quickly, and thanks to the creation of the Canadian Railway Corps in 1915 – a body that by the end of the war had 16,000 men in France – by June 1916 the extent of the light railway

Above: Britain came late to field railways, first deploying them in numbers from 1916, and the wounded being evacuated here on the Somme offensive are being hauled by a petrol-driven Simplex locomotive, which was far less visible to enemy forces. The open wagons have received impromptu modifications to accommodate stretcher cases, and the standard-gauge tracks next to it suggest the train is near an interchange point.

Next page: Railway construction continued on all fronts, with new spurs and even new routes being built to serve the armies.

had increased to 315 miles and, with the commencement of the Somme attacks, by September that figure had reached 700 miles. The Canadians were railway builders *par excellence* and they were eventually given responsibility for laying field railways across the British sector. Their expertise was critical in supplying the British and Commonwealth front lines.

DIFFERENT RULES

The field railways operated very differently from their standard-gauge equivalents. There was neither the time nor the need to build a comprehensive signalling system and timetable for these railways – flexibility was one of their greatest strengths and so communication was by telephone. Provision was made for trains to pass in opposite directions at loops along the routes from the railheads, with officers pausing trains as required.

The field railways had their limitations, however, and this tended to dictate how they ran. For most of the war the locomotives were steam-powered and that restricted operations to night-time as the readily visible plumes of smoke, as we have seen, revealed all too easily in daylight where the trains were running. Rush hour was invariably from 6 p.m. to 6 a.m. and as dusk approached trains loaded with ammunition and other supplies were prepared at railheads: when it was considered dark enough to operate safely they set off towards the front lines one after the other.

Without any signalling to ensure a safe distance between them they were driven 'on sight', the drivers only being required to ensure they left enough distance between the train in front to stop safely. With low speeds – 10mph was the fastest they could safely operate on lightly laid track – this was

Right: At the Battle of Ypres in 1917 British soldiers unload shells from a field railway in preparation for an artillery barrage. Empty shell cases are ready for transport back from the front lines.

a reasonably acceptable way of working and one that maximised the carrying capacity of the railways. Keeping the telephone lines intact was the job of the signalling sections of the respective armies and this was a constant task. Not only were the lines liable to be severed by shelling, but marching along the tracks themselves was often the easiest way for soldiers to reach the front and they were constantly damaging the fragile telephone wires as they did so.

Accidents were frequent: runaway wagons and derailments occurred every single night and though breakdown crews were on hand to restore service it was often the driver, fireman and guard of a train – with any soldiers they were transporting – who had to manhandle the rolling stock back on to the rails. The locomotives presented a trickier proposition but, with just this sort of mishap in mind, they were invariably fitted with jacks. With muscle power primitive tools and the old standby of soldiers in all armies – swearing – the trains continued to run in often appalling conditions.

Despite popular imagination, the field railways

arely went to the trenches themselves – they may
ave been small railways but they weren't *that* small
nd the sounds of the railway would carry across no-
nan's-land too easily for safety even at night: a steam
ocomotive at the front line was a visible and easy
arget for enemy artillery.

With greater experience in the use of field rail-
vays so the handling capabilities also increased, so
nuch so that by June 1917 260 tons of freight was
arried per week over each mile of route operated
n comparison to 100 tons in December 1916. A

contemporary 3rd Army order illustrates the importance that was now being attached to the light field
railways in the British sector alone: in the French and
German lines they were equally vital. In terms of importance siege and heavy shells were to be dealt with
first, then light ammunition, followed by engineers'
materials, rations, ordnance stores etc. Wounded men
returning from the front lines were to be given pref-
erence to other traffic at all times and by all sides.

In January 1916 light railways were responsible for
the carriage of 1,300 tons of stores of all types per day
and a few RE working parties. By the end of September the lines were carrying 20,000 tons of stores
and, most significantly, 30,000 men per day. Carriage
of such volumes of traffic would not have been
possible under the old ad hoc style of organisation;
now the BEF no longer regarded the narrow-gauge
railways as a mere 'tramway' adjunct but as a fully
integrated component of the main system managed
and run by experienced railway personnel.

The 60cm tramways used at the very front and
invariably employing mules rather than locomotives
were vital last transport outposts for many aspects
of the army operation, too. Shells removed from
ordnance dumps were delivered to heavy artillery
batteries on hand trollies over light and often ballasted
tramways and the wounded were carried back from
forward positions by the same method. Transference
of shells to the lighter field artillery batteries was often
more problematical given that these units were closer
to enemy fire. In these cases delivery of shells was increasingly made from dumps situated along points of
the more distant light-gauge railways by road vehicles.

Left: *Canadian soldiers await evacuation after their attack at
Vimy Ridge on 9 April 1917. The tracks in the background
illustrate the flexibility of the field railway system – likely to
be used to extend the railway towards the front, these panels
could be lifted and laid using manpower alone quickly and
with little preparation of the ground.*

Through operation from the tramways to the light railways and vice versa, although enabled by the use of the same gauge, was often non-existent to prevent the non-return of the latter's rolling stock. Although a few connections were eventually made, particularly at points that were under enemy observation and shellfire, junctions and transfer points between the two remained few and far between. The transhipment between standard-gauge and field railways was inevitable but a huge drain on manpower. The armies effectively had free labour to undertake these tasks but this represented a significant diverting of manpower from the front line, and even Britain and the Commonwealth were struggling to source enough troops by 1917, such were their losses on the Western Front and commitments elsewhere. In response to this pressing need the British administration at the Wei-Hai-Wei coaling station in northern China recruited more than 40,000 Chinese labourers to work on the field railways. Thousands more served the Allies for little pay, working long hours to release soldiers to the front. Their efforts are now almost forgotten but without them, the trains wouldn't have kept moving.

After the start of the Third Battle of Ypres (otherwise known as Passchendaele), which began on 31 July 1917, an exercise was mounted by the British that August to see if the light railways were delivering some of the prime objectives set out in the first months of their use – to relieve the roads of slow-moving and damaging lorry traffic, the ability to aid an infantry advance across an area of land badly damaged by shellfire and the speedy conveyance of road materials to areas requiring reinstatement or resurfacing. Given the appalling weather during stages of the Ypres offensive it was little short of a miracle that the light railways had reduced the demand for lorry traffic in a period that would normally have seen a great increase in their use. Even this couldn't prevent localised counter-attacks seizing field railway systems and both sides were quick to connect enemy

networks to their own to support their advances. Captured equipment was used extensively – the common gauge meant that wagons were easy to use against their original owner; locomotives less so as providing spare parts was obviously a problem – but while they were operational there was no hesitation in using them to supplement existing rolling stock.

TECHNICAL DEVELOPMENTS

The Germans and the French both had standardised designs for locomotives and wagons. Germany started the war with 250 of the brilliant 'Brigadelok' 0-8-0 tank engines, built mainly by Orenstein & Koppel and the famous locomotive builder Henschel.

The numbers describe the configuration of a steam locomotive: the first refers to the number of unpowered leading wheels that guide a locomotive around curves (where there were none, 'O' was used to signify this); the second (and in some cases third where articulation and separate sets of cylinders were used) the driving wheels which provide traction, and the final number the trailing wheels under the cab to support the weight at the rear and provide additional guidance. More than 2,000 'Brigadeloks' were built during the war, supported by 500 0-4-0Ts, 300 0-6-0Ts and 40 impressive 0-10-0Ts.

France had developed and manufactured Péchot-Bourdon 0-4-4-0T articulated locomotives, which were powerful, reliable and could ride the rough track easily, and 330 or so were built during the war, but French industry was almost entirely focused on armaments manufacture and so turned to Britain to supply narrow-gauge locomotives. The North British Locomotive Company in Glasgow built Péchot-Bourdon locomotives, and Britain's other independent locomotive builders moved quickly to fill the gap – and their order books – with other designs. Kerr-Stuart supplied 0-6-0Ts based on Decauville's designs, but still it wasn't enough, and this presented both the French and the British with a real

challenge in acquiring sufficient locomotives for the field railways. They turned to the United States and that country's vast locomotive building industry was able to deliver the steam engines the Allies needed so quickly. Baldwin Locomotive Works quickly came up with a 4-6-0 tank locomotive and built 495 of them. Shortcomings in this design – notably its tendency to derail and rough riding – led to a standard 2-6-2T, which was built in vast numbers by the American Locomotive Company (ALCO), too.

The development of the internal combustion engine inevitably led to rolling stock builders investigating whether it could be applied to railways. For the big standard-gauge railways the early engines simply weren't powerful enough to do a useful job, but on the field railways, whose trains were much lighter

and slower, even a 20hp machine could be effective. The advantages were obvious: with no steam and smoke emitted they could work much closer to the front lines while remaining invisible to the enemy. The German company Deutz developed a range of highly successful four- and six-wheel petrol locomotives, but it was Britain that eventually gave most thought to using internal combustion engines on the field railways. It even investigated the use of overhead wire-powered electric locomotives but as the first petrol 'tractor' locomotives entered service their

Above: A French 164mm fires north on the enemy at Noyon, France, probably in 1918 following the German advance which pushed the French back towards Paris.

success rendered any such ambition irrelevant. A host of British companies, including British Westinghouse, Dick, Kerr & Co., Motor Rail Tractors and Ernest E. Baguley tractors, provided the means for the Allies to get supplies that little bit closer to the front lines than was possible with steam traction. The Americans, too, lent their industrial muscle to the effort, Baldwin supplying its own 50hp 'tractor' to the field railways – initially to France and then, after the US entered the war, to its own forces.

A GLOBAL CONCEPT

Field railways undoubtedly reached their apogee on the Western Front but everywhere armies relied on trains for transport the little trains ran. Inevitably the Germans used them on the Eastern Front (mostly in Poland), as did Austria-Hungary in Galicia and the Russians wherever they could. The Russian army was also able to benefit from the use of the Decauville 60cm- and 75cm-gauge systems. It laid more than 1,243 miles of field railways, with locomotives supplied by its own Kolomna Locomotive Works and ALCO. Baldwin, too, supplied 350 750mm gauge petrol locomotives for Russian service. With such poor standard-gauge railways on much of the Eastern

UNDER FIRE AT AUDRUICQ

' On the morning of 21 July 1916 German aeroplanes came to pay the camp at Audruicq a visit and
dropped bombs on the ammunition yard. This was a
very large yard full of sheds stocked with every kind
of ammunition from 12-inch shells to rifle ammunition and trench mortars of all kinds used in warfare.

Their bombs set fire to the stacks of cases in the
sheds and in a very short time the place was all in
flames and shells and other explosives were bursting
and flying all over the place.

The whole of our camp, which by this time had
grown to considerable size, was destroyed … this
took place at 1.15 a.m. when nearly all the men
were at rest. So quickly did it spread that large
numbers of men only had their underclothes on and
had to escape as quickly as possible.

The situation in the ammunitions yard was getting
very serious as the sheds containing the heavy stuff
caught fire and terrific explosions were taking place
and showers of metal were falling in all directions.
The steel rails were torn up and flung in all directions and wheels were torn from axles and tyres
off wheels. This was going on all the day and night
until there was not a shed or railway wagon left in
the whole yard.

Church windows for miles around were shattered
and hardly a roof or pane of glass was left in the
town of Audruicq. The country for miles around was
laid to waste. As our camp had disappeared we were
billeted in the village of Nortkerque until they could
get fresh tents and stores.

When the ammunition started to fire some drivers
and mates off the yard shunting engines took refuge
in a dugout. When Major Barrington-Ward heard
of this he took an engine and driver into the yard
and at great risk rescued the men from their dangerous position. He was awarded the DSO and the
driver the DCM for bravery … it was estimated
that some 37,000 tons of ammunition and 400
railway vans had gone up. One crater in the yard
was torn 60ft deep. '

Sergeant C. Webster, Carmarthen (from IWM C.E.R.
Sherington Collection)

Front the field railways played an important role for all sides with the sheer distances involved – more so in some respects than their shorter counterparts on the Western Front. There were never enough of them to exert a decisive influence, however: they may have been comparatively quick to build but neither side could afford to divert the manpower from the fighting forces it would have needed for truly comprehensive networks.

Plans for building field railways in the Allies' failed attempt to force the Dardanelles at Gallipoli in 1915 had been developed and material stockpiled was used to reinforce the defences of the Suez Canal while the standard-gauge railway across the Sinai Peninsula was built, and in Italy it and Austria-Hungary used a mixture of field railways, tramways and cable cars to supply forces in the mountainous South Tyrol region where so much of the fighting took place.

When a Franco-British force landed in Salonika at the request of the Greek Prime Minister in October 1915 to help the Serbs against Bulgaria and Austria-Hungary it was field railways that supplied the troops. Built in haste to support a tricky and often bogged down operation against tough opposition, the field railways in this often overlooked theatre allowed the Allies to keep enough soldiers and supplies flowing to avoid a repeat of the debacle at Gallipoli. The difficulty of building and extending existing standard-gauge railways in the region led to a series of lengthy field railways being built (the biggest, from Stavros to Gvesne, was just over fifty-eight miles long). Operation was made more challenging by fuel shortages and the limited endurance of the little locomotives, but they showed what was possible.

Throughout 1916 and 1917 rail networks had been developed and extended on all fronts, with the field railways increasingly to the fore in the west. Their role, on all sides, was vital. They had their limitations, as we have seen, and might even be regarded as a necessary stop-gap solution while road transport matured – but without the field railways France, Germany and Britain in particular would have fought a very different war.

REVOLUTION

It was a completely different train journey that set the tone for events of 1918. The February revolution in Russia was a direct response to food shortages, high inflation and war weariness of military and civilians. Tsar Nicholas II abdicated on 15 March, his unpopular rule replaced by a provisional government which exerted little if any authority over huge tracts of Russia. With America declaring war on Germany in April 1917 and heavily engaged industrially for the Allies long before then, the Germans colluded with Lenin and other Russian revolutionaries to allow him to return to his homeland from exile and secure a Communist revolution. He travelled in disguise through Germany, in what became known as 'The Sealed Train', with the full knowledge of the Kaiser's government, passing through Berlin, crossing the Baltic to neutral Sweden and then into Finland, which was then part of Russia. He arrived in Petrograd on 16 April to a hero's welcome. Over the following months he worked against the provisional government and in October 1917 widespread unrest exploded into full-blown revolution. Russia was in chaos, unwilling and unable to continue fighting Germany. It would give the Kaiser a last shot at victory before the arrival of vast American armies made defeat almost inevitable.

Right: Even funicular railways were used to support the military in mountainous areas. They were often the only practical way of transporting soldiers and supplies into the mountains – particularly on the Italian Alpine front.

9

GERMANY'S LAST GASP

GERMANY'S LAST GASP

Russia's October revolution and moves to secure an armistice with Germany gave the Kaiser one last throw of the dice and his generals were quick to seize the opportunity. They knew full well that their only remaining chance of victory was to defeat the Allies before the overwhelming resources of the United States turned the balance of military power against them.

Germany released fifty divisions from the Eastern Front to give it a temporary superiority in numbers on the Western Front, and her only option short of a major offensive – attempting to broker peace talks from a position of strength – was rejected on the grounds that the Allies would be unlikely to accept anything less than a complete victory culminating in what would today be termed unconditional surrender.

Planning was begun to launch a massive offensive designed to eliminate one of the Allied forces, which in turn would pressure the others, if not the initial target of the attacks, into breaking their treaty terms and sue for peace. The decision was taken at a conference on 11 November 1917 at Mons in Belgium – where Germany had first engaged the BEF in August 1914. When to attack was easy to decide – as soon as possible after the winter weather of 1918 had cleared – but the best location was less obvious. After much debate it was decided to select the sector near St

Quentin adjacent to the old Somme battlefields and extending up towards Arras. Tactically it made perfect sense. Here, at the junction of the British and French armies, the opposition was weak, the ground better and drier than in other sectors and the opportunities for a rapid success to be transformed to one of major strategic implication more likely. Once the 'crust' of the front line had been broken the aim would be to penetrate further and then 'roll up' the British front from the south, either destroying it or forcing it back upon the Channel ports. Once Operation Michael (as it was known) was launched, the idea was to keep the Allies off balance with additional attacks aimed against British sectors to the north and also against the French further south. The scope of the plan was breathtaking but, as in 1914, it made fatal assumptions about the enemy's reactions and capabilities.

The Allies knew that a German attack was imminent: on 3 December 1917 Haig summarised his thoughts on the likely events in the forthcom-

Above: Field Marshal Sir Douglas Haig, Commander-in-Chief of British Empire forces, on the Western Front, in his headquarters train. The train wasn't a luxury, as the cramped office shows – but it was by far the best and most effective means for Haig and his staff to travel around the Western Front, liaise with his generals and remain in communication while being effective.

ing calendar quarter to his five army commanders. Admitting that the army was understrength, with few reinforcements and suffering the consequences of having to despatch five divisions to Italy from early November, he stressed the inevitability of a defensive attitude in the coming months: 'We must be prepared for a strong and sustained hostile offensive … and army commanders should give their immediate and personal attention to the organisation of the zones for defence and to the rest and training of their troops.'

The Allies couldn't know precisely where the attack would fall but with numerical advantage now with the Germans it was one they were bound to

make use of. Throughout the war defence had never been a strong point in British military planning but now some radical and very speedy rethinking had to be done. Given the paucity of British field strength, flexibility would be vital in resisting the Germans should they attack the British sector. Throughout the

winter of 1917/18 new training programmes were begun and a completely new defence methodology set up behind the established front lines. The front line proper was now classified as the 'Forward Zone', or 'Blue Line', and regarded as merely an outpost line but held in sufficient strength to attract the attention of German artillery, inflict casualties upon the attackers and then effect a retirement to a 'Battle Zone', or 'Red Line', some 2–3,000 yards to the rear. Here, robust defences advantageously placed would carry on the fight – hopefully to a successful conclusion. Further back were the 'Brown' and 'Green' lines, offering further defence zones and where the reserves could be held until they were needed in the event of any part of the 'Red Line' being breached by the enemy.

Plans, too, were made to ensure that even soldiers hitherto not destined for combat were prepared. 1st Army Light Railways troops were issued with rifles and bayonets and trained in their use. Plans were drawn up for the evacuation of the field railway locomotives and wagons and clear briefings given to ensure the safety of staff and, if necessary, the demolition of facilities to deny them to the enemy.

By the beginning of March, Germany had assembled nearly a million men in seventy-nine divisions within the rear areas virtually without a hitch and completely undetected by Allied reconnaissance. Jump-off areas, gun positions and additional railway facilities in the forward areas were prepared only

Left: In a posed picture, in 1917, American Secretary of War Newton Diehl Baker sits with generals Pershing and Walsh in what is claimed to be an Active Service Conference. The real conference would have taken place indoors and probably not on a train.

Next page: The British supplied the Great Central Railway designed '8K' heavy freight locomotives to France in numbers from early 1917. This locomotive has just been delivered as it awaits its Railway Operating Division insignia, and a mixture of British troops, ROD staff and French railwaymen pose in front before it takes up its duties.

by night and during the day German aircraft were instructed to fly over the sectors to ensure there was no sign of undue offensive activity.

From 9 March German units began to move forward, usually by day and by train. The men were told nothing of the plans but many could work things out for themselves. The 27th Division had trained in Alsace and on completion of training boarded trains at Colmar. After passing through Strasbourg the trains headed west and only then did soldiers know they were bound for the Western Front. On reaching their forward positions the men were forbidden any movement outside during the day.

DEFENCE IN DEPTH

Thanks to German success in concealing the location of the forthcoming attack, the British had to spread their efforts to install the new defences across the full extent of their front. The area to the north around Ypres was always the BEF's priority and so it was here that it concentrated its resources, with the other sectors suffering a subsequent diminution as the front moved further south. At the very last moment, when it became clearer that the German attack would be concentrated much further to the south, in the 3rd and 5th Army sectors, the extra resources that were thrown in were too little and, with so much work still to be done, almost too late.

Unlike in 1914 the British had not neglected their support operations. The railway construction companies of the Royal Engineers had been expanding their operation with the construction of 814 miles of track of all gauges throughout 1917, almost double the amount of 1916. The first of the railway operating companies raised in April 1915 and deployed to France had expanded massively in numbers and remit. They were now tasked with management of railway traffic, provision of footplate crews for locomotives and the repair of rolling stock and other items needed to keep a railway in operation on the

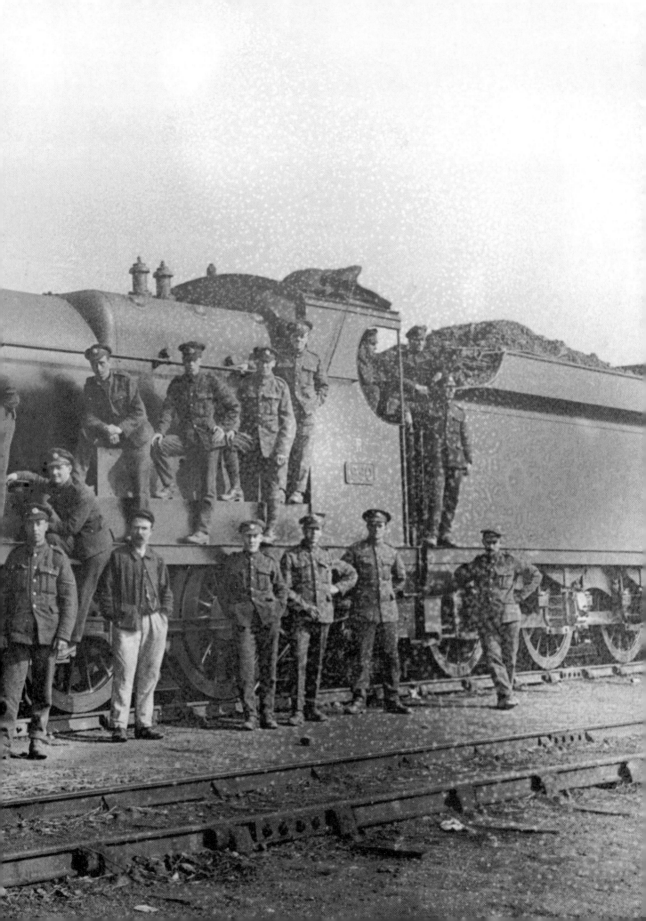

standard-gauge railways in northern France, which were increasingly coming under British control.

BEF locomotive crews had to learn the local routes and also pass Belgian and French signalling examinations before they were allowed on the routes. ROD locomotives were also subject to Belgian and French railway inspection. Each company, known as 'Broad Gauge Operating Companies' (to distinguish them from the field railway operations), had a contingent of RE officers, NCOs and sappers and also contained ninety-two drivers, the same number of firemen and associated railway trades such as boilersmiths, blacksmiths and various fitters.

In the north of the BEF sector, where trench lines were sixty miles or less from the coast and with the now extended front line to St Quentin bringing up the front-line length of the BEF to about 120 miles, the route distances might be considered short by railway standards but for the British to be operating them at all reflected the strain being placed on France's railway network and its depleted reserves of men. From early 1917 the ROD became responsible for the haulage of an increasing mileage of Nord Railway traffic, including civilian services, in order to relieve pressure on the French resources. Miners' trains in the Béthune area were also powered by ROD engines. And some of these routes were risky, too. Speculative shelling from the German lines occasionally damaged the railways, and aerial bombing and strafing was another growing hazard. Railway movement often had to take place at night under blackout conditions, adding another aspect of danger to even the most basic railway functions.

By 1917 troop trains had been standardised into a single coach for officers, thirty covered vans of the 'Hommes 40 Chevaux 8' variety, seventeen flat trucks and two brake vans which together could carry 1,200 men or 240 horses. Communications had improved massively since 1914 and now British Commander-in-Chief Douglas Haig and his staff had the use of

a special train of eleven converted London & North Western Railway sleeping carriages and three vans, one of the latter fitted out as a communications centre and two others for stores and a train heating unit. This might smack of generals living in luxury behind the lines while their soldiers fought and died in the trenches but it was a pragmatic and sensible move: it was vital for Haig to be able to travel along the front and meet his commanders and he also needed to be able to plan effectively. Only a train could provide the mobility the General Staff needed when away from permanent headquarters with facilities for work and rest.

In early 1917 two sets of four trains were established around Béthune and Amiens as a mobile operational reserve with each having the capability of moving a brigade-strength army unit inclusive of its transport facilities. Daily supply trains running along the main railway routes sufficient for two army divisions comprised thirty wagons containing rations, horse fodder and petrol, two wagons of coal, four of ordnance of one type or another, two wagons of mail and two brake vans. For an average of sixty divisions in the line at any one time from 1916 onwards, at least thirty supply trains were needed daily at the main railheads for transhipment to the light railway system or road transport – and there were also trains switching supplies and troops between divisions. The movement of local or tactical trains within army areas or to another neighbouring army was inevitably subject to variation. Main lines in rearward areas could be used for between forty and sixty trains per day but on routes closer to the front this number might well drop to between sixteen and twenty-four. It all added up to a very sizeable railway operation by any standards.

The growth of the Railway Operating Division had been rapid: in 1917 eight large depots were taken over or constructed and an ever-increasing mileage of the French railway system used for BEF services

rought under their control. The numbers of ROD
ocomotives in service – many from Britain and in-
luding some of the latest types, such as the versatile
43XX' 2-6-os built by the Great Western Railway
nd the '8K' 2-8-0 heavy freight engines developed
·y the Great Central – grew from seventy-two
·1 April 1917 to 267 by December while services
·perated over French lines grew from a mere ten in
·Aarch 1917 to 314 in October. In early 1918 addi-
·ional standard-gauge lines solely under ROD control
·ad also been opened in the 3rd Army sector to avoid

French traffic restrictions imposed on BEF services
on trains from Amiens.

In the soon to be critical area of the 3rd and 5th
Army, standard-gauge main lines were minimal. There
was a network of military lines built by the French
in 1915/16 but these had been left behind when the
Germans pulled back to the Hindenburg Line in

Below: A British wiring party passes a rail-mounted gun at
Arras. The gun seems to be rather closer to the front lines than
would be normally considered acceptable.

early 1917. There were only two standard-gauge lines covering the twenty-four miles between Péronne and Noyon which encompassed the old front line and the new in late 1917 – the main Amiens–Tergnier line and a secondary line from Ham to St Quentin. With the assumption that British forces would remain permanently in the area, considerable effort would be needed to bring it up to a satisfactory transport level for military needs.

By 1918 the ROD had the capability to move two divisions simultaneously on twenty-four trains over a twenty-four-hour period. One movement sequence would take in the French coast railway from Calais–Boulogne–Etaples and then to Abbeville and Amiens. The other route would take in the route from Hazebrouck to St Pol and Arras and thence to Amiens. Reserve divisions were based where there were good entrainment facilities, and their destinations, except *in extremis*, had similar provisions. It all sounds obvious today, but the availability of railway infrastructure was dictating the day-to-day deployment of armies on both sides of the front lines.

Railway plans to combat the expected German spring offensive had three phases – firstly, the initial attack stage upon the 'Blue Line' where the strength of the BEF was already known and its supply requirements already recorded; secondly, the development of the attack and the likely occupation of the 'Red Line'; and, lastly, the possibility of the 'Brown' and 'Green' lines being breached and the movement of reinforcements from other armies (including the French) into the area in order to counter-attack.

Although army plans for railway supply in the event of an offensive could be expressed in series of known values (three trains daily for each division and

Right: *As the campaign developed the British took the lead in providing alternatives to steam traction. This petrol locomotive was deployed as early as 1916 – and, with no tell-tale plume of smoke, could operate much closer to the front lines than steam locomotives.*

Above: The standard-gauge rails may only be 1,435mm apart, but they could carry vast loads. The limitation of guns like this on 25 June 1918 was their slow rate of fire – far less than conventional howitzers.

two and a half for a supporting division, for example), the formula for defensive actions was less clear and entirely dependent on enemy action.

In the 5th Army zone the daily supply train requirements were organised as a half-train for each division and another half-train per corps, four trains for all types of ammunition and a further five for all other purposes. Ambulance train evacuations were expressed as a requirement for six trains to be availa-

ble within six hours of the opening of the attack (Z day) with a further eight within the first twenty-four hours, twelve more on Z+1, and another twelve on Z+2 sufficient for up to 16,000 casualties. Ensuring uninterrupted supply of ammunition and the replacement of damaged or destroyed artillery pieces was subject to much fine-tuning. Shell and ammunition dumps held up to 20,000 tons of *matériel* at any one time and the daily expenditure was calculated at around 12,000 tons. The dumps were arranged in two lines so that if the first was overrun there was a second to fall back on. After the first two days of the expected attack it was calculated that nineteen trains per day would be required for shells of all calibres nd one for small arms and grenades to keep up with expenditure. On average, each railhead would need to handle up to 2,000 tons of ammunition per day, which required extremely close coordination between each train's Railway Transport Officer and the Railhead Ordnance Officer responsible for clearing the trains and railhead reception points for onward transport up the line. As a last resort instructions were issued for the destruction by the Royal Engineers of the permanent way and the infrastructure in the event of the possibility of these falling into enemy hands.

The British were rushing to prepare for a German attack and in March the situation of the ROD infrastructure within the 3rd Army sector had improved notably. A standard-gauge line from Miraumont to Le Transloy was nearing completion and many new 60cm-gauge lines had also been opened across the areas of the old Somme battlefields of 1916. The situation behind the 5th Army sector showed similar progress and much effort had been put into improving the rail facilities there. A new connecting standard-gauge line connecting the Péronne–Chaulnes and Etricourt–Fins lines had been completed, three new railheads installed and many new 60cm extensions to the existing system added. In the final analysis, though, while the soldiers were given clear briefings and training about how to deal with the German attack, the railways which supported them would have to think on their feet and improvise as the attack developed.

THE LAST THROW

On 21 March the expected blow fell on the 3rd and 5th Army sectors. After a storm of three million gas and high-explosive shells lasting five hours, thirty-two German divisions attacked a weak and extended BEF two-army strength of twenty-nine divisions, of which only one battalion of each brigade was holding forward positions. The results were immediate and

impressive. Within less than an hour of the start of the infantry attack the specially trained storm-trooper units had exploited the shock of the bombardment and the unexpected bonus of fog to infiltrate or overwhelm British lines along a distance of fifty miles. From the northern sector of the 3rd Army down to the southern extremities of the 5th Army and its border with the French 6th Army at La Fère, victory seemed to be complete. By nightfall the Germans had inflicted over 38,000 casualties on the British alone, of whom 21,000 had been taken prisoner.

In many areas the 60cm lines were overrun and the speed of the attack necessitated the withdrawal by rail of many large-calibre artillery batteries to prevent capture. In one 3rd Army position the battery commander refused to allow his guns to be moved until a locomotive was brought up to take them away. The position was under fire and the track had been cut in several different places. Only after considerable effort and loss of life was the battery saved. Demolition of railway bridges was undertaken but with a decision to do so taken by the man on the spot – usually a fairly high-ranking Royal Engineer officer who would often delay matters until the arrival of stock on the 'last train' from the front and with the enemy in sight.

There was much rail movement of troops within and between the army areas of influence and particularly the delivery of shells. In one day the 3rd Army reported the requirement of no fewer than eighteen trains to keep pace with expenditure. As the rapidity of the advance increased the ROD also needed to deal with far more evacuations of unskilled labour from the railheads, civilian evacuees and also civil and French military authorities than it could ever have expected. While the military traffic over the standard-gauge lines of the Nord increased enormously, at the same time demolitions of the main lines near the threatened parts of the front were also taking place as well as dismantling railway workshops at Longueau and Amiens.

In the 5th Army area where the German advance was the speediest destinations of ROD trains had to be changed en route to avoid possible interception and destruction. On 23 March Péronne fell and by the 26th all lines worked by the ROD east of the Arras–Amiens main line had been evacuated and the prearranged railheads lost, requiring a withdrawal to other sites further west. A further evacuation of the Albert–Arras main line worked by the Nord also became imperative at the same time and the ROD had to be hurriedly drafted in to evacuate a battery of railway guns at Boisleux because of the hasty departure of the French authorities.

It could have been chaos but the British had learned quickly in almost four years of war. Although ground had been lost and headquarters shifted frequently, here at least Germany's offensive was beginning to run out of steam as the age-old problems of casualties, exhaustion and supply mounted and began to sap the resolve of the attackers. A last attack by the Germans on 24 April took Villers-Bretonneux, but with Amiens on the horizon the attack finally ground to a halt. A counter-attack the following day recaptured the town and the British lines, although battered beyond recognition, had nevertheless held. The German breakthrough had failed.

Meanwhile, events moved further north with the opening of a second series of attacks against 1st Army on 28 March and then heavier and more penetrative assaults on 9 April and against 2nd Army a day later. On 11 April Haig issued his famous 'backs to the wall' order of the day against a background of further German advances and it was feared that without substantial French reinforcements the Germans could advance the remaining fifteen miles or so to the Channel ports within the week.

But, once again, quick thinking and pre-planned controlled retirements to established railway-fed defence lines ensured that no major breakthrough occurred. Experience gained from the rapidity of the southern attacks had resulted in the establishment of railheads further back than those of the 3rd and 5th Armies and these were now brought into use. Some of the coalfields of the Béthune area were threatened and all rolling stock from affected collieries was also withdrawn. Pre-planned evacuation of *matériel* from stores and dumps at Strazeele and also from the local ROD HQ at Merris was begun where 400 wagons were recovered within hours of the attack commencing. The speed of the attack saw German forces capture two supply trains and a railway gun in the 1st Army sector, but despite this all other standard and 60cm rolling stock was recovered. The evacuation plans had worked.

The repair shops and stores of the ROD at Borre, a mile east of Hazebrouck, were ordered to be evacuated as a precautionary measure, as were the light railway workshops at Berguette. As the compression of the British forces increased in the northern sectors the ROD facilities at Audriucq and Zeneghem were under enormous pressure to deal with the increase of evacuated lines of communication equipment. By 14 April 21,000 tons had already been dealt with and further equipment was pouring in at the rate of 2,000 tons per day. Controlled evacuations of ammunition dumps by the ROD continued and where it was not possible to achieve this in many cases the ordnance was issued directly to artillery units which had taken up positions close by. German attacks continued and Kemmel Hill to the south was lost as well as Armentières and the gains painfully achieved from the previous year, including Messines Ridge and most of the enlarged Ypres Salient. However, French reinforcements in divisional strength detrained at Gravelines, Dunkerque and Bergues and bolstered the battered British divisions positioned along the new defence lines running through St Omer.

By late April 1918, the danger of a German breakthrough had passed. A dent had been made in the British lines but once again they had not broken. The

A RAILWAYMAN'S VICTORIA CROSS

John Meikle, the young clerk from Nitshill station in Glasgow whom we met in Chapter 4, was one of the thousands of railwaymen who served in the armed forces who didn't survive the war. Meikle, by now a sergeant in the 4th Battalion of the Seaforth Highlanders, died on 20 July in the Second Battle of the Marne in the Ardre valley. Aged just twenty when he died, and having already won the Military Medal at the Third Ypres in 1917, his citation reveals this young man's bravery. His father, John, was presented with the medal on 28 October 1918 at Maryhill Barracks, Glasgow, the place his son was sent to upon enlistment in 1915.

His citation reads:

Award of the Victoria Cross
No. 200854 Sgt. John Meikle M.M. late Sea. Hrs.
(Nitshill)
For most conspicuous bravery and initiative when his Company, having been held up by machine gun fire, he rushed single handed a machine gun nest. He emptied his revolver into the crews of the two guns and put the remainder out of action with a heavy stick. Then, standing up, he waved his comrades on.

Very shortly afterwards another hostile machine gun checked progress, and threatened also the success of the company on the right. Most of his platoon having become casualties, Sgt. Meikle siezed the rifle and bayonet of a fallen comrade, and again rushed forward against the gun crew, but was killed almost on the gun position. His bravery allowed two other men who followed him to put this gun out of action.

This gallant non-commissioned officer's valour, devotion to duty and utter disregard of personal safety was an inspiring example to us all.

He wrote a poem in March 1918 that is barely known today. It may not stand comparison with the literary greats of the war, but it came from the heart.

I fought in a battle to-day, mother,
The enemy's fire was strong,
The shrapnel screamed overhead, mother,
And shrill was the bullet's song.

And after the battle was o'er, mother,
And I had time to rest,
I felt so sick and sad, mother,
My heart was so depressed.

I longed to be safe, in the fold, mother,
So I fell on my knees in the mud,
And I prayed to God above, mother,
'Oh wash me in Jesus' blood'.

Just as I said these words, mother
Sweet peace pervaded my soul,
I knew God answered my prayer, mother,
That he'd cleansed and made me whole.

So rejoice with your wayward lad, mother,
Who has found his god at last;
Who after your loving prays, mother,
Into Light and Life has passed.

Meikle lies in the British cemetery at Marfaux. A memorial to him was unveiled at Nitshill station in January 1920 and removed to Dingwall, where the 4th Battalion was formed, in 1971.

Left: John Meikle, VC, a railwayman from Glasgow, is commemorated in this memorial at Dingwall. A ceremony was held at the station he worked at, Nitshill, on 24 April 2014, with schoolchildren and the Southwest Scotland Railway Adopters Group planting poppies in his memory.

German attacks stalled again because of heavy casualties, supply problems and the threat of counter-attacks upon the exposed flanks of their new salient, while the British had successfully covered the approaches to the Channel ports and kept contact with French forces to the south. The ROD had kept supply lines open under constantly changing situations, moving troops and reinforcements with the minimum of notice and, where evacuation was necessary, successfully achieving most of this, including the removal of all the railway-mounted heavy artillery.

A NEAR VICTORY

On 27 May a final effort was made to break British and French defence lines between Soissons and Reims. Here, the defence lines had not been developed and there were no adequate reserves to launch counter-measures. As a result the front collapsed and, although British and French units were able to contain any development on the flanks of the new salient, German troops advanced once more as far as the River Marne; as in 1914, Paris seemed about to fall. Yet once again the German army fell victim to the same elements that had stifled the attacks further north, which resulted in substantial tactical gains but zero strategic success.

The Americans fought in force and fought well, defending the Marne crossings at Château-Thierry, and, as in previous attacks, the rear defence mechanisms involving transportation of men and materials invoked a system of 'lignes de Rocade' trains. The name comes from the French term for the castling move in chess and is a reflection of the lateral movements required to redistribute supplies and army units from one army area to another, or to and from separate army supply bases. Such moves were orchestrated across fully equipped block system-worked double-track railways as non-stop services with the elimination of any time-consuming reversals or shunting at junctions.

By 1916 four such routes had been established between the south bank of the River Somme and the French border with Switzerland. Three of these routes took in Amiens – the key centre of operations in the summer of 1918 and one of the most important rail centres anywhere in the First World War – perhaps *the* most important. By the end of 1916 three similar routes had also been established, running up from Amiens linking Arras, Calais, Dunkerque and Hazebrouck.

With Foch now Allied supremo, throughout 1918 the use of these routes increased and became instrumental in the ability of the Allies to move units quickly, efficiently and at short notice in response to German activity. French units could be moved into British sectors, British units into French ones and reserve armies assembled as the situation demanded. Using this method the Allies were able to respond to the German attacks on the Somme by moving no fewer than forty-six divisions in twenty days during the second attack in Flanders, twenty-nine during April and early May and, for the last attacks culminating in the Second Battle of the Marne, sixteen French and two American divisions. If chess was the miniature embodiment of the art of war then this railway strategy of the movement of pawns and knights in full scale was the living proof of it. French railway operation and the thinking behind it was nothing short of brilliant. The parallels with 1914 were stunning, the exception being Britain's much larger and more capable forces, and the expectation now was of a gruelling war of attrition that would continue into 1919.

TIME TO BREATHE

After the impetus of the German attacks had faltered the front entered a period of relative calm, which allowed the Allies to regroup. The French railway system had become very run-down and, with the arrival of increasingly large numbers of American troops and their additional supply needs, extra strain was imposed on the system. To assist, the ROD took over the complete operation of more lines in the Doullens, Fervent and Hazebrouck areas. Also making their presence felt was the arrival of many American Locomotive Company (ALCO) and Baldwin 2-8-0 locomotives for the use of the American railway troops but a number of these became available for the ROD. American industrial might was making itself felt on the standard-gauge railways as well as on the battlefield.

With the successful stabilisation of the front, the gradual assimilation of fresh American forces and the rehabilitation of an effective defence scheme of movement behind the front, Foch turned his attention to the notion of a vast counter-offensive to push back German forces. On 8 August the first phase was launched. Three hundred and forty-two tanks followed up by British, Australian and Canadian troops punched an eight-mile hole in the German defences, prompting the German commander, Ludendorff, to declare it 'the black day of the German army in the war'.

In this he was correct but it would be followed up by another one hundred of them as the Allies began slowly but surely to push the German army back to a line that, for the British at least, would end up where they started in 1914, at Mons.

For the Amiens attack, the ROD had conveyed seven of the nine tank battalions into position in great secrecy. By using the 'Rocade' system to best effect, moving troops only at night and feigning movements during the day to mask their true intent, the divisions used in the attack (two British, two Australian, three Canadian and elements of the American 33rd) were also in place for the assault without arousing German suspicions. The complete success of the attack marked the beginning of a series of withdrawals by the German army and the process of renewed attacks by the Allies to keep a now off-balance enemy

on the back foot. The recovery of railway lines, their restoration and the re-establishment of supply railheads now became a daily challenge for the ROD as the Allies advanced steadily eastwards.

Although the ROD had by this stage established six main feeder lines to the front from Dunkerque, Calais, Boulogne, St Quentin and Laon, the pace of the advance beyond the available supply railheads was so rapid in some areas that these were left far behind – in some cases up to twenty-five miles in the rear of the assaulting troops. It was a reversal of the German advances of 1914 and 1918, and supply had to revert to lorry transports which further damaged the roads and slowed the pace of the advance – though lorries themselves were more numerous, reliable and capable then they had been just four years before. With the rapid withdrawal of German forces from the Marne, these distances extended to up to forty miles with transport struggling to keep up with the advancing troops.

As was now widely understood, it was very difficult for railways – and particularly the supply dumps on which the army depended – to deal with a rapid advance. The ROD had to contend with the destruction of railway facilities, particularly large bridges and station and yard facilities. On the 4th Army front, for example, the demolition of the large 200-yard (183m) -long, 80ft-high railway viaduct at St Benin, near Le Cateau, posed a major problem of reconstruction. The obvious alternative of building a deviation, normally a temporary workable solution, in this case would take up to three weeks to engineer and was no solution to the supply problem. Added to these problems was that of delayed action mines which were often detonated after lines were brought back into service.

For the ROD it was a slow and frustrating period. Although many vital routes such as the Arras–Douai, Hazebrouck–Armentières, Maricourt–Péronne and Chaulnes–Péronne lines had been brought back into service, many of these were capable of carrying only a fraction of their potential because of the temporary nature of the repairs. The need always was to get some trains running as quickly as possible on the principle that anything is better than nothing. But one of the many consequences of the fragility of the recaptured railways was the army's decision not to attempt to bring up the heavier artillery pieces and railway gun units to add weight to the advance. In September railheads were still receiving huge quantities of ordnance – indeed, in the same month an average of up to thirty-five ammunition trains a day were arriving – but increasingly their delivery to batteries was slowing as distances between them increased, exacerbated by the often minimal availability of light railway supply.

As the forward momentum continued the ROD also found it increasingly difficult to match their own progress and in many sectors, particularly those where there had been so much devastation of the ground and demolition of the rail and road infrastructure, the advance often slowed to the speed of a mule train. Accidents in temporary sections increased and air attacks by the still active German air force were another factor to contend with, all of which added a delaying factor into the mission of supply.

The need was to consolidate the gains, bring the supply networks forward and then prepare for the next forward lunge. Winter would inevitably bring major fighting to a halt, and, as November 1918 approached, the Allies grimly but determinedly prepared for a major offensive the following spring.

At the end of the war the ROD personnel complement numbered 18,500, including forty-eight standard-gauge operating companies, an engine crew company plus six workshop companies.

ERIC GEDDES

Eric Geddes was born at Agra, India on 26 September 1875. He travelled to the USA in 1892 and undertook a variety of jobs, including as brakeman on freight trains and assistant yardmaster on the Baltimore & Ohio Railway.

After a spell in India managing part of a steam tramway and later working as traffic superintendent of the Rohilkhand and Kumaon Railway, he returned to England in 1904 to join the North Eastern Railway under its traffic apprenticeship scheme and was promoted to chief goods manager in 1907, and then to Deputy General Manager in 1911.

Kitchener summoned him to a meeting in December 1914 to discuss railway facilities in France, and from May 1915 he was deputy director of munitions supply, playing a key role in resolving shortages of munitions, for which he was knighted.

But it was his railway role which was most important and, after being asked by Secretary of State for War, Lloyd George to 'put transport right in France', Geddes visited General Haig who appointed him director-general of transportation in France with the substantive rank of major general. Geddes centralised transport operations in a headquarters known as 'Geddesburg' and instituted the large-scale construction of field railways and better standard-gauge facilities for the British armies.

In May 1917, when submarine warfare was inflicting huge losses on Allied shipping, he was appointed Controller of the Navy with responsibility for Admiralty docks and shipyards.

Post-war he was famed for the 'Geddes Axe', which saw swingeing cuts to public spending and left politics in 1922 to become Chairman of Dunlop Rubber and part-time Chairman of Imperial Airway. He died at his home near Hassocks, Sussex, on 22 June 1937.

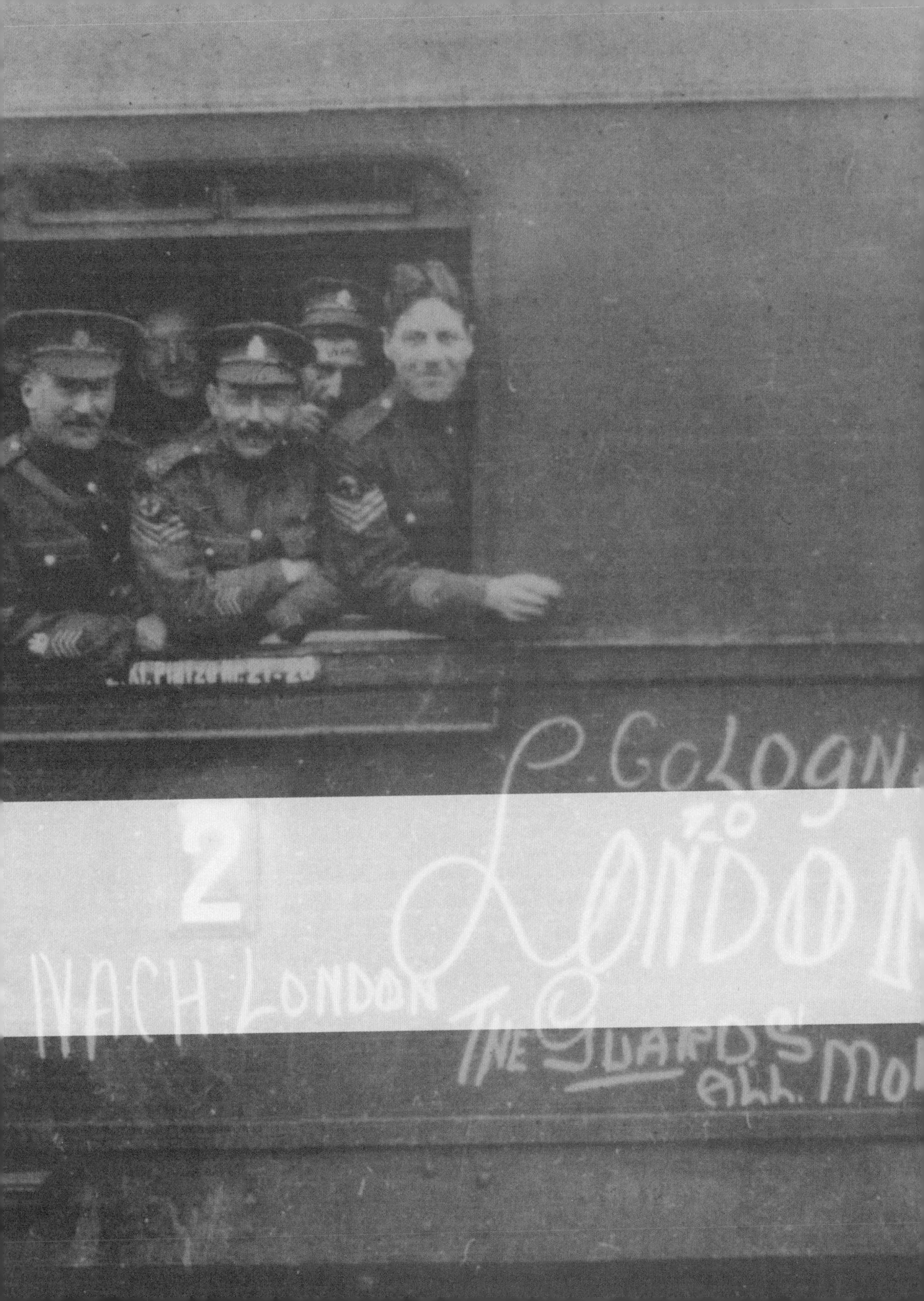

TO
LONDON
2
NACH LONDON
THE GUARDS'

10

THE AFTERMATH

THE AFTERMATH

In the end, the First World War was indeed over before Christmas, as many had predicted, but it was Christmas 1918 rather than 1914. With the fighting having ended in most places the railways were still needed to feed troops, return prisoners and help rebuild shattered economies. The effects were profound.

Suddenly it was over; across the battle wastelands, wrecked towns and villages the dissonance of artillery gunfire gave way to birdsong and the efforts of man and nature beginning the slow process of reclamation. The trench network of the combatants of the Western Front alone was estimated to have stretched 25,000 miles – enough, if it had been a single trench, to encircle the Earth. A hundred and seventy million shells had been fired by the BEF since August 1914 and the German army had returned an equivalent number. Some villages had virtually disappeared, replaced by a landscape more reminiscent of the Moon than of Earth.

For many soldiers the sudden reversion to peace within a shattered environment was oddly disturbing. Yet for soldiers of all sides, one feature of the conflict remained as a link to the recent past: the sight and sound of steam locomotives and their smaller narrow-gauge brethren still performing their missions of supply across the former war zones.

There was no sudden decision to stop fighting: it was more a dawning realisation that internal pressure within Germany and Austria-Hungary meant that the war was unwinnable. By the beginning of November, while Germany was still actively attempting to find a practical and face-saving way out of the war, the Austro-Hungarian Empire had been slowly fragmenting and there was no time to broker a favourable deal.

On 27 October, Austria approached the Allies independently for an armistice and at the same time ordered its army to give ground. Two days later the Serbs, Croats and Slovenes proclaimed the establishment of a southern Slavic state, to be called Yugoslavia, while the Czechs and Slovaks of Bohemia and Moravia proclaimed the establishment of Czechoslovakia as an independent state. After many years of partitioning Poland re-emerged as an independent country, the Second Polish Republic.

On 30 October, an Austrian delegation arrived in

ARRIVAL OF ARMISTICE COURIER AT SPA

The Daily Mirror

CERTIFIED CIRCULATION LARGER THAN THAT OF ANY OTHER DAILY PICTURE PAPER

No. 4,695.   Registered at the G.P.O. as a Newspaper.   MONDAY, NOVEMBER 11, 1918   One Penny.

DEMOCRACY TRIUMPHS OVER LAST OF THE AUTOCRATS

The Kaiser and his son need not bid each other good-bye. They are both going the same way.

The crowd in the Mall awaits news of the enemy answer to Allies' armistice proposal amid the thickly-ranked guns captured by the British in the final battles on the western front.

Above: The Daily Mirror marks the Armistice on 11 November 1918.

Italy to offer unconditional surrender. On the same day Hungary formally declared its independence. On 3 November, all the terms of the Austrian armistice had been agreed, and it was signed the following day in a modest villa at La Mandria, on the outskirts of Padua, bringing an end to the Austro-Hungarian Empire after 114 years of turbulent history. The name of the property, the Villa Giusti, subsequently gave its name to the armistice.

On 14 October 1918, Mehmed VI, last Sultan of the Ottoman Empire, having suffered heavy territorial losses since 1917 and now facing the threat of a British invasion of Turkey proper, requested peace terms. It was confirmation of a prophecy written in a letter found on the body of a Turkish officer at Gallipoli in 1915. The unfinished letter contained the sentence 'We have chosen the wrong friends' and neatly summed up his country's dilemma.

An armistice was signed between Britain and Turkey at the port of Mudros on the Aegean island of Lemnos on 30 October and it brought to a close the Ottoman dynasty and an empire that stretched back to 1453 with the conquest of Constantinople. Much of the Ottoman territory outside Turkey was to be dismembered, to re-emerge as independent countries but shackled as British, French, Greek and Italian 'spheres of influence'. Within a few years this would be the cause of much renewed conflict. In 1920, with the prospect of a Greco-Turkish war imminent, Winston Churchill pithily summed up the situation: 'At last,' he said. 'Peace with Turkey: and to ratify it, war with Turkey!'

By November 1918 and with Germany riven by internal political chaos, riots, a lack of foodstuffs and, since 29 October, bereft of the Kaiser, who had sought refuge at army headquarters in Spa, Belgium, the situation facing Chancellor Prince Max von Baden was desperate. Paul von Hindenburg, the *de facto* leader of Germany, had long since recognised the inevitability of an armistice – but on what terms? On 29 September the Kaiser had agreed to open negotiations with President Woodrow Wilson on the strength of his famous 14 Points and had espoused a new parliamentary regime and universal suffrage in order to give a democratic façade to the martial exterior of his country which, it was hoped, would gain them points at the negotiating table. A note was sent by von Baden to Wilson asking him '... to take in hand the re-establishment of peace and to conclude an immediate armistice on ground, sea and in the air'. However, despite the positive tone of the message and its apparent willingness to concede, there was much disagreement among the Allies as to the final shape an armistice would take.

On 7 November, just before his resignation, von Baden finally despatched a group of German delegates by train to a secluded location of Compiègne, in northern France, to negotiate an armistice. But by now, despite Wilson's conciliatory attitude, the Allied stance had hardened, especially so since the capitulation of Austria and Turkey. Hindenburg's parting words to Matthias Erzberger, the German Secretary of State and armistice delegate, were a reflection of

Right: *Rebuilding the shattered railways of north-east France and Belgium was a massive effort which saw the British, French and Belgians restore services amazingly quickly. The town of Arras was devastated and its station was no exception.*

how the situation had deteriorated: 'Go with God's blessing and try to obtain as much as you can for our homeland.'

Germany had hoped to be able to negotiate from a position of relative strength rather than be forced to accept whatever demands the Allies chose to make. Now, with Germany on the brink of insurrection, von Baden was forced to concede that he had no choice but to sue for the best terms he could get. The delegation arrived on the morning of 9 November, and the negotiations began promptly. The same day, Prince Max took the step of announcing Wilhelm II's abdication – without the now delusional Kaiser's agreement (he finally confirmed his abdication on 28 November after his arrival in the Netherlands) – and then himself resigned, leaving separate left-wing political groups to fight over the body of a now prostrate Germany.

THE ARMISTICE

Finally, on 11 November, at 0510, the armistice with Germany was signed. Hostilities officially ceased at 1100 that day. On the eleventh hour on the eleventh day of the eleventh month the shooting stopped.

For Germany, it was a day of complete humiliation. The country was required within fifteen days to evacuate the occupied areas of Belgium, Luxembourg, France and Alsace-Lorraine and also (and impossibly, it has to be said) the repatriation of all the inhabitants of these countries. The German army was to surrender 5,000 artillery pieces, 25,000 machine guns, 3,000 *Minenwerfer*, 1,700 aeroplanes, 150 submarines and, of course, the High Seas Fleet. The left bank of the Rhine was to be evacuated of all units of the German army and replaced by Allied garrisons. Crossings of the Rhine at Coblenz, Cologne and Mainz were to be guarded and garrisoned with extra troops. Communications of all types were to be handed over to the Allies and also a vast quantity of railway hardware to make good the losses of

Belgium, France and to a much lesser extent Britain (whose confined loading gauge at home made it impossible to use much German rolling stock even if it had wanted to). Five thousand locomotives, 150,000 railway wagons and 5,000 lorries were to be delivered within thirty-one days and the railway system in Alsace-Lorraine handed over. Other stipulations were more straightforward and included the repatriation of all prisoners of war, the whereabouts of all mines and delayed-action devices in the battle zones, the right of the Allies to requisition in the occupied areas, and all military areas to be left intact. (The German High Seas Fleet later countermanded this order by taking its own initiative and scuttling its ships in Scapa Flow on 21 June 1919.)

In the space of a few weeks the world map had changed profoundly. Austria-Hungary was split up into Austria, Hungary and Czechoslovakia; Bosnia Herzegovina, Croatia, Slovenia, Dalmatia and Vojvodina were merged to form what became Yugoslavia, and the newly created state of Poland was granted Galicia and other parts of Austria-Hungary. Romania gained Transylvania and Bukovina, while Italy won Trieste and the southern part of the Tyrol.

Germany saw large swathes of East Prussia handed over to create Poland and lost the port of Danzig to further create a Polish corridor to the sea, although the city was legally an independent city-state with customs union with Poland. It lost control of the Rhineland but retained East Prussia, though this was cut off from the rest of Germany. In the Middle East, the Ottoman Empire's former possessions were carved up to create the states that for the most part remain today; in Africa Germany's possessions were split between Britain, France, Belgium and Portugal, and in Asia, too, Germany lost its empire, with Japan, New Zealand and Australia taking over.

THE ALLIES IN EUROPE

The BEF, although no longer needing vast quantities

ÉDITION DE PARIS

Le Petit Parisien

10 Cent. — LE PLUS FORT TIRAGE DES JOURNAUX DU MONDE ENTIER — 10 Cent.

MARDI 12 NOVEMBRE 1918

"LE JOUR DE GLOIRE"

L'acte de capitulation signé hier par l'ennemi met fin à la guerre

L'APOTHÉOSE

TRIOMPHAL HOMMAGE DU PARLEMENT
à M. Clemenceau
à Foch, à tous les chefs, à tous les soldats

LE LIBÉRATEUR, CLEMENCEAU

LE VAINQUEUR, FOCH

L'AGRESSEUR EST ABATTU

Félicitations de M. Poincaré aux combattants de la grande guerre

LES CONDITIONS, LES GARANTIES

Left: Unsurprisingly, the French newspaper Le Petit Parisien *of 12 November 1918 was overjoyed but was surprisingly low key in its celebrations. The French would later seek revenge at Versailles.*

Right: Marshal Foch of France (centre) poses just after the signing of the Armistice with the signed document in the satchel under his arm. On his right is the British naval representative First Sea Lord Sir Rosslyn Wemyss.

of ordnance, still required clothing, food, mail and the upkeep of the logistics of movement. Strung out on many routes across Belgium and northern France towards the German border and the allocated zones of occupation, many thousands of troops were still reliant on the services of the ROD. British troops, along with their Belgian, French and American allies, occupied the Rhineland. The British were allocated the city of Cologne and surrounding area and the occupation was intended to last for fifteen years, with the number of troops being reduced in stages after five and ten years.

In the other direction trains carrying horses for repatriation, servicemen on leave and surplus equipment headed for the Channel ports and, within weeks of the cessation of hostilities, demobilisation reduced the numbers of BEF servicemen from an all-time high of over three and a half million to just under one million a year later.

Prior to the Armistice the evacuation of occupied territories and the return of railway facilities to their former owners provoked much thought among the authorities. Many hundreds of miles of track would instantly be added to systems in Allied hands whose resources were already stretched to cope with what they had. It was of paramount importance that sufficient manpower and material were left behind by the Germans to man and equip the recovered systems. Railway staff were ordered to remain at their posts and Belgian and French railway workers were to return to their former jobs whether they had been interned or not.

The 5,000 locomotives and 150,000 railway wagons (together with spare parts where needed) demanded of Germany were to be delivered along with crews to operate them, giving Belgium the means to restore services quickly. The railway divisions of the Allied armies continued to work the railways in Belgium they had taken over, while in France the existing arrangements would continue for an inter-

Above: Demobilisation took a long time, and many troops were sent to Germany to occupy the Rhineland. In 1919 troops head back home, this time with the certainty that they will reach the destination chalked on the carriage sides.

im period. In Germany, a joint railway commission representing Britain, France and the United States would operate the railways west of the Rhine.

The plan was for Belgium to receive around 80,000 wagons and France the remainder, and in recognition of the fact that its railway had lost 2,500 locomotives since 1914 (600 operational locomotives had been left by the Germans) they received 400 German locomotives initially, to be shared with France. Five hundred were allocated for British use but in the

be of the most powerful types. Belgium eventually received 168 of the very latest and successful Prussian P8 4-6-0 class introduced in 1906, while France received 162. Greece, Italy, Lithuania and Romania each received quantities of this type, with 627 of these brilliant locomotives alone leaving Germany.

Permanent replacement of lines and facilities across the devastated battle zones remained a problem with much of the hasty and temporary reconstruction work imposing speed and weight restrictions on the limited number of trains which could be worked. However, by the end of January 1919 sufficient progress had been made in crossing the band of devastated country to achieve satisfactory supply levels required by the armies of occupation in Germany.

In early February the ROD was able to return to the Belgian railway authorities all of the principal lines in Belgium previously worked by the British. For a time ROD personnel were retained on the railways to oversee and assist operations but by the end of March all had gone, leaving a residual number of ROD engines continuing to work Belgian services into April. The return of lines belonging to the French Nord Railway was similarly scaled down. In February 1919 the company took back the operation of all its lines still totally worked by the ROD and then the running of their own trains which had been powered by ROD stock. By the end of February the Nord had taken back virtually all of its operation and at the same time traffic on much of the British military lines had also ceased. It was, in a sense, 'all quiet on the Western Front'.

From a loftier pinnacle Churchill said of the conflict:

'Every institution almost in the world was strained. Great empires had been overturned. The whole map of Europe has been changed. The position of countries has been violently altered. The modes of thought of men, the whole outlook on

event most of these were sent straight to Belgium. As early as January the ROD had enough locomotives sent over from Britain to allow them to return rolling stock borrowed from Belgium since 1915.

It was stipulated that the types of locomotive to be handed over must be of the 'most powerful types', which posed an immediate supply problem. Germany insisted, correctly, that the terms of the Armistice article made no such provision and the ruling had to be amended to allow that only 1,000 of the total should affairs, the grouping of parties, all have encountered violent and tremendous changes in the deluge of the world.'

CIVIL WAR IN RUSSIA

After Russia's 1917 revolution its railways became a key tool for the Communists, linking regional soviets and allowing them to counter opposition. After the collapse of the Brest-Litovsk agreement in March 1918 Russia descended into civil war and the armoured trains that fought on the Eastern Front against the Germans were now used by both sides to win an advantage. The Red Army itself built more armoured trains, the number rising to around 100 by 1920 and all saw extensive action. The Czech Legion, largely formed of prisoners of war, rebelled against the Bolsheviks and took over the Trans-Siberian Railway, capturing armoured trains supporting the fragile White regime based in Vladivostok. For a time armoured trains engaged in the railway equivalent of dogfights, acting as railborne tanks, but gradually the Bolsheviks applied the lessons learned by the British in the Boer War and used them as mobile bases with supporting infantry and cavalry to great effect. By 1922 the Russian civil war was effectively over with the Bolsheviks in charge. It was the last time armoured trains would play a major role in any conflict.

CHANGES IN BRITAIN

In Britain three million families had lost a family member – a father, a husband or a son – and it is understandable that people began to refer to the recent conflict as the 'The War To End All Wars' and to attach the popular slogan 'Never Again' to it. Politically, Lloyd George and his coalition party hastened to cash in on the chips accumulated since 1916 with the so-called 'Coalition Coupon' Election of 14 December 1918. 'The coupon' was a disparaging reference made by Herbert Asquith to the letters of endorsement signed by Lloyd George and Conservative

Party leader Andrew Bonar Law sent out to selected parliamentary candidates endorsing them as official representatives of the coalition government. Those receiving the coupon were seen by the electorate as patriots who had supported the government during the war, while those who did not were regarded as anti-war or pacifist. The 'Coupon Election' was the first in which women over the age of thirty who owned property, were graduates voting in a university constituency or who were on or married to a member of the Local Government Register could vote, as well as all men over the age of twenty-one. Although polling was held on Saturday, 14 December 1918, Lloyd George delayed the count until 28 December because of the time taken to transport votes from soldiers serving overseas.

The coalition won the election easily, with the Conservatives the big winners, but Lloyd George was once again elected Prime Minister.

Almost immediately the new government was faced with the severe economic cost of the war. From being the world's largest overseas investor prior to 1914, it had now become one of its biggest debtors with interest payments peaking at around 40 per cent of all government spending. Inflation had also been on the increase since 1914 and would more than double in 1920.

In addition, demands suspended since the beginning of the war by the railway unions for the introduction of an eight-hour working day and a national pay scale had been presented at the government's doorstep almost immediately after the cessation of hostilities. Although the question of pay scales remained unresolved for a while, the support of Albert Stanley, the President of the Board of Trade, helped to ensure the eight-hour day was introduced on 1 February 1919, marking a significant success in the unions' long struggle against excessive hours.

Herbert Walker, ex-Chairman of the REC, was later to comment on its introduction as 'possibly the

THE MEMORIAL LOCOMOTIVES

Britain's railways had named many of their steam locomotives almost since the dawn of the railways and after the Great War three British companies – the Great Central (GCR), London, Brighton & South Coast (LBSCR) and the London & North Western (LNWR) – honoured railway staff who died in the war with cast memorial plates fixed centrally to the splasher panels of selected engines.

The LNWR already possessed various locomotives named in honour of distinguished Great War leaders and crowned heads: even nurse Edith Cavell, executed by a German firing squad in 1915, was not forgotten. Key events such as Gallipoli (notably Suvla Bay) and Anzac, as well as the loss of certain ships – among them the *Lusitania* – were also marked.

In January 1920 the company named one of its flagship 'Claughton' express locomotives *Patriot* in honour of those 3,719 former employees killed in the war. Appropriately numbered 1914, the locomotive's nameplate was a large centrally mounted plate of simple design with the legend 'In memory of the fallen L&NWR employees 1914–1919' underneath.

The Great Central Railway followed in July that year by naming one of its brand new express locomotives, No. 1165, *Valour* to honour its 1,304 war dead. It had a distinctive shield-shaped nameplate inscribed with the additional words 'In memory of GCR employees who gave their lives for their country 1914–1918' on the locomotive splasher panel and incorporated within the line of the decorative beading edge.

The third company to opt for a memorial locomotive was the LBSCR which in 1922 selected the express tank locomotive No. 333. It was the last member of its class to be built and the last by the company before the grouping of 1923. A single nameplate *Remembrance* was fitted to the side tanks with a second plate mounted below carrying the inscription 'In grateful remembrance of the 532 men of the LB&SC Rly who gave their lives for their country, 1914–19'. The locomotive was soberly painted in grey with black and white lining bands with lettering and numerals that were white blocked in black.

Across the other side of the world one further locomotive was given similar treatment. This was a member of the 'AB' Class of 4-6-2s built for New Zealand Railways in 1925. No. 447 was chosen to commemorate the 447 railwaymen killed overseas during the conflict. The name given was *Passchendaele* – a place of tragic significance in New Zealand military history. The nameplate was enclosed within a wreath of floral bordering and contained the words 'In memory of those members of the New Zealand railways who fell in the Great War 1914–1918'. It survives to this day.

Although the British steam locomotives were long ago scrapped, the name 'Patriot' lived on an electric locomotive running on the West Coast Main Line until 2005, and the names of regiments and historic events have continued to appear on British locomotives. There has never been an 'official' memorial locomotive, but it is hoped that in 2018 a replica locomotive of the 'Patriot' class (the original locomotive was later rebuilt to this form) will be in operation to mark the centenary of the end of the Great War. The £1.5 million locomotive will be numbered 5551 and named *The Unknown Warrior* in memory of all service men and women who died in the First World War.

wickedest thing that had ever been perpetrated on a community'. In effect the railways had to increase staffing levels by some 12 per cent to compensate for the reduction of hours per man.

Agitation for a national pay scale continued with the added union proviso that the war bonuses of up to 33s. (shillings) per week should be incorporated within the new standard rates of pay. This, they argued, was needed to counteract the effects of the spiralling cost of living – particularly for employees in lower paid grades. Negotiations dragged on for some while but matters seem to have been resolved in August 1919 when the unions accepted a plan to regularise footplatemen's wages with the inclusion of the war bonus. However, when the government placed its final wages settlement plan for other railwaymen grades in September these employees were to lose their war bonus and be paid an amount equivalent to their 1913 rates. In effect the weekly wage of porters would drop by 11s., guards by up to 7s. and ticket inspectors by up to 10s. The National Union of Railwaymen (NUR) rejected the proposal and a strike commenced on 26 September. The locomen grades joined the NUR in support and a vigorous appeal for public support through the pages of the national press was launched.

The railwaymen had by far the most convincing case and, far from them being (as the Establishment would have it) a collection of anarchists, Bolsheviks and revolutionaries, it was obvious that they were fighting for a reasonable standard of living. The public were all too aware of the contribution made by railwaymen to the war effort. With the distinct possibility of other non-railway unions coming out in support with their own independent actions the government backed down and the strike ended on 5 October. Lloyd George agreed that wages inclusive of war bonuses should remain at their present levels until September 1920 and that no railwayman should receive less than 51s. per week as long as the cost of

Above: *The Armistice was signed in a railway carriage which was the personal coach of Allied Commander Marshal Ferdinand Foch. In 1940 Hitler used the same carriage to receive the French surrender to Nazi Germany.*

Next page: *Britain's railways and those of New Zealand marked the sacrifice and dedication of its soldiers, sailors, airmen and railwaymen by naming locomotives. The most famous was the London & North Western Railway's 'Claughton' 4-6-0 express engine No. 1914, named* Patriot. *A new project to recreate a version of the locomotive in its rebuilt form is hoped in 2018, and will be named* The Unknown Warrior.

living did not fall below 110 per cent of pre-war rates. In effect it meant that a porter on 49s. per week would receive a rise of 2s.

Eric Geddes, as Minister of Transport and infamous for his quip 'squeezed as a lemon is squeezed – until the pips squeak' aimed at the German people, hardly endeared himself to the railwaymen when he attempted to withhold pay for the week leading up to the strike. Geddes had received a £50,000 golden handshake from the North Eastern Railway and even the *Daily Mail*, a vocal critic of the strike, was moved to publish a headline instructing him to 'Pay Them What They Have Earned'.

The conclusion of the war saw the British railways, if not actually on their knees, then saddled with an accumulation of much needed track and rolling stock maintenance work and the consequences of staff shortages. Some 184,000 men had joined the colours since 1914 and of these 18,957 lost their lives. A slight amelioration of the locomotive stock was achieved with the return of many of the British locomotives loaned for war use in France and with the purchase of numbers of the standard ROD 2-8-0 freight locomotives. The Great Western Railway bought 20 of the class in 1919 and a further 80 in 1925, while the LNWR bought 30 locos in 1920 with a further 75 of the class purchased in 1927. The largest purchaser of the ROD engines was the soon to be created London and North Eastern Railway (LNER) which bought 273 between late 1923 and early 1927 to supplement its 130 existing GCR Class 8K locos.

In 1914 the government had promised to return the railways to the same state of health they were in when they were taken over at the start of the war. The railways had not been allowed to increase fares in line with inflation and although passenger fares had risen by 50 per cent in 1917 and by a further 25 per cent after the war it was still not enough. Even worse, given that freight was the lifeblood of the railways, freight charges had remained fixed since 1913.

In January 1919 Eric Geddes was tasked by Lloyd George to organise a new Ministry of Transport with a remit to take over all transport affairs from the Board of Trade. With added clout as first Minister of Transport from May 1919, Geddes's new department came into existence on 19 August 1919.

In particular, the central control of the railways was to be relaxed by August 1921, which would allow sufficient time for the planning of the change that many recognised as the first whiff of nationalisation. Almost immediately Geddes came under severe criticism for the size of the new ministry and the salaries of some of its top staff. Criticism was also levelled at the way some of the interim compensation claims from railway companies were being handled. One particular claim from the North British Railway (NBR) for a perfectly justifiable £616,000 was deemed as needing further investigation and only £186,000 was paid out. Legal infighting eventually came down in favour of the Ministry and the NBR had to wait for its money until state decontrol. The case was evidence, if any were needed, that vast sums in claims were to be expected from the railways – figures as high as £400 million had been quoted. In the event the companies received a total of £60 million, not even half the amount they were owed.

Announcements that passenger fares and freight tariffs were to be increased by 100 per cent in July 1920 proved controversial, but it was a nettle that the government had to grasp in order that the railways could be legally released from state control with anything like an even chance of profitability resembling that of 1914. The current total income compared to that of 1913 was short by an estimated £54.5 million and there was little time to redress the balance.

The increases had the effect of driving business, particularly freight, to a growing number of road haulage entrepreneurs who were already benefiting from the cheap availability of vast numbers of army surplus vehicles. There was widespread anger at government claims that the railways were subsidised and must pay their way – it was their cooperation with the government during the war, including producing munitions at cost, which had made Britain's war effort possible. Britain's railways were being stabbed in the back by the very government they had done so much to support.

There were calls for nationalisation but in the end the government decided to merge Britain's myriad private railway companies into four groups – the Great Western, London Midland & Scottish, London and North Eastern, and Southern Railways.

A FORMAL END

The Treaty of Versailles formally ended the state of war between Germany and the Allied Powers and after much argument and negotiation was finally signed on 28 June 1919, exactly five years after the assassination of Archduke Franz Ferdinand. It required Germany and her allies to accept the responsibility for causing all the loss and damage during the war. This clause, known as Article 231, later became known as the 'War Guilt Clause'. The treaty forced Germany to pay reparations to certain countries that had formed the Entente powers. In 1921 the total cost of these reparations was assessed at 132 billion Marks, or £6.6 billion. At the time many economists stated that the treaty was too harsh and the reparation figure both excessive and counter-productive.

Because of the lack of reparation payments by Germany, France occupied the Ruhr in 1923 to enforce payments. This sparked an international crisis resulting in the implementation of successive payment plans that would, in theory, see the debt cleared by 1988. However, with the collapse of the German economy in 1931, reparations were suspended for a year and then in 1932 cancelled altogether.

The treaty was signed after months of argument and negotiation among the so-called 'Big Three' of Lloyd George of Great Britain, Clemenceau of France and Woodrow Wilson of America. On the surface, Lloyd George's stance was predictably simple. The prevailing mood of 'Hang the Kaiser' and 'Make Germany Pay' was one that he could not afford to ignore. However, in private he was also very concerned with the rise of Communism in Russia and feared that it might spread to Western Europe once the war had finished, posing a far greater threat than a defeated Germany. With this in mind he believed Germany should be treated in such a way that left her as a barrier to resist the expected spread of Communism. He did not want the German people to become so disillusioned with their own government that they turned to Communism. In contrast to Clemenceau, who wanted Germany brought so low as never again to be capable of waging war, Lloyd George had no desire for a destitute Germany that would render her incapable of resisting a 'red tide'. Woodrow Wilson, while stunned by the savagery of the Great War, did not seek a large role in European affairs, preferring an arm's length involvement towards reconciliation as opposed to revenge.

The League of Nations, founded on 20 January 1920 and based in Geneva, was an international organisation created to provide a platform for resolving international disputes. In many ways it was an antidote to the conflicting threads of the Treaty of Versailles and had one simple aim – to ensure that global conflict would never again occur. The League enjoyed some notable successes in the 1920s in areas such as the Aaland Islands of Finland, Upper Silesia, Memel (a humanitarian crisis resulting from conflict in Turkey), and a border dispute between Greece and Bulgaria, but was powerless against the successive European flashpoints that led up to the events of September 1939.

AMERICA'S RAILWAYS – ARMING THE ALLIES

By 1914 the railways of the United States had long been the glue that held together the vast nation since the end of the civil war in 1865. It was the only form of transport that could guarantee speed and accessibility and the bulk movement of goods across thousands of miles of territory before the automotive age. Huge areas of the country, notably the Mid-west, the former lands of the Native Americans and, more recently, Florida, had also been opened up and harnessed to the burgeoning industrial might of the north-eastern states.

Heavily populated cities were further boosted, some even owing their survival to the arrival of the railways, and many new towns sprang up along the routes where commercial potential could now be fully realised. In return, the railways were able to stimulate industry with a soaring demand for coal, iron and timber in order to maintain the increment of its spread and technological progress as well as their own transportation ability.

Many aspects of British practice had been observed and followed throughout the years, most notably the adoption of standard gauge by the late 1880s – a measure of huge significance in the future American railway war effort at home and abroad.

One feature not common to British practice at the time was the degree of state intervention in regulating the rates charged by the railway companies and limiting certain questionable and monopolistic business practices employed by some of the entrepreneurs who had made fortunes from their railway investments. In 1887 Congress created the Interstate Commerce Commission (ICC) and further legislation followed in 1906 increasing its regulatory powers over the railway companies, including the seven large corporations which controlled two-thirds of the rail mileage of almost 165,000 miles.

That mileage figure had increased to 254,000 by the time the United States entered the First World War and before long it was obvious that the network was struggling to keep up with the demands of the nation's war effort. Because of the insistence of the ICC to limit prices, many companies found it difficult to operate at a profit let alone invest in necessary improvements.

Inadequate infrastructure facilities such as outdated freight terminals and a lack of modern rolling stock in places added further problems to a system bedevilled by the negative effects of competitive practices and the conflicting demands of government departments bent on securing preferential treatment for their respective war shipments. Congestion and chaos was added to freight yards and harbour facilities already under severe pressure. In *The Great Railway Revolution: The Epic Story of the American Railroad* the railway historian Christian Wolmar observed, 'the railway companies failed to understand the imperatives of wartime, even if America was not directly involved until April 1917'.

Strikes by the unions plagued the industry before the war, putting a further brake on operational efficiency. Industrial action was threatened again in 1915 and 1916 for shorter working days and better pay and was only averted by the passage of the Adamson Act, which set the eight-hour working day as the industry standard.

By autumn 1917 operational matters reached a head with an estimated shortage of 158,000 vehicles, and considerably more than that number saturating the eastern seaboard ports waiting to be transhipped. (This wasn't helped by Germany's unrestricted U-boat campaign which, although it had waned somewhat since earlier in the year, was still sinking around 300,000 tons of shipping every month.) In December that year the ICC recommended federal control of the industry, bringing railway labour, management, investors, and shippers under one national interest umbrella.

On 26 December 1917 'nationalisation' became a reality with the creation of three new operational divisions: East, South and West. Terminals, yards and depots became common user installations, passenger services and ticketing were streamlined and duplication of formerly competing services ceased or substantially reduced. In addition, almost 2,000 new standard steam locomotive designs and over 100,000 freight cars were ordered.

To put the industrial effort in context, Baldwin Locomotive Works produced 5,551 engines of various types for the Allies, gun mounts for the US Navy, two million Enfield rifles subcontracted from Remington and no fewer than 6,565,355 artillery shells for Britain, Russia, and the US Army and this was just one company! It was a prodigious effort.

Taking its cue from the British example, in March 1918 the Railway Administration Act became law, guaranteeing the return of the railways to their former owners within twenty-one months of the restoration of peace. The Act also stipulated that the companies' assets would be returned in at least as good a condition as they had been when they were taken over and compensation would be paid for their use at a rate equivalent to the average operational income of the railroads in the three years prior to the 1917 nationalisation.

Although there was support for nationalisation once the war had finished, Congress passed the Railroad Transportation Act of February 1920, which ended government jurisdiction over the railway companies but retained and increased ICC's powers over the railroads, giving extra powers of approval over mergers, rates and closures.

TRAINING AMERICA'S WAR RAILWAYMEN

In northern Virginia an army railway camp at Fort Belvoir, known as Camp Humphreys, was set up in 1918 to train soldiers in the skills of combat engineering and railway practice. After the United States declared war on Germany on 6 April 1917, Camp Humphreys became an important mobilisation training area for sappers and in early 1918 its role was extended to include a twenty-mile, 2ft-gauge railway comparable to those systems used by British, French and German forces to supply munitions and troops from the standard-gauge railways to the front-line area.

From March 1918 until the end of the war hundreds of soldiers and engineers trained on the little Camp Humphreys railway, learning how to put together the track, build railway trestles and operate the locomotives safely and effectively.

Camp Humphreys was not alone in running the two-foot gauge systems: similar facilities were installed at Fort Benning, Georgia, Fort Sill, Oklahoma, Fort Benjamin Harrison, Indiana and Fort Dix, New Jersey, among others, and some of these remained in place for another generation. However, by 1920, the system at Camp Humphreys had been dismantled, its wartime application over.

Next page: American recruits board their train at Woodhaven Junction, Long Island, on their way to military induction at the nearby Camp Upton shortly after the United States entered the war.

CONCLUSION

There is a tendency for all writers of history to immerse themselves in their period and to imagine what it might have been like to have been in a particular situation themselves. They believe, as do I, that it is essential to do this in order to understand the events they are writing about.

It seems a statement of the obvious to say that railways were important to the nations fighting the Great War – given how vital they were in their civilian roles, it was inevitable that they would play a major role in the conflict. Even so, a number of aspects stand out which perhaps haven't attracted the attention they deserve in wider military histories.

Firstly, although planned years in advance, Germany's mobilisation to its borders in 1914 was a brilliant example of railway planning and operation. So, too, was Russia's speedy deployment of troops to the Eastern Front, helped admittedly by the deployment of substantial numbers of troops in Poland. France's use of railways on the defensive in 1914 was a genuine masterpiece – perhaps the most outstanding of all in the war. Without the ability to move fresh troops about quickly (and in good condition) France might well have lost the Battle of the Marne. Without France's rail network the Great War may well have been over by Christmas 1914.

Belgium's spiriting away of rolling stock and the denial of its railways to Germany in 1914 deserves credit, as does Turkey's stubborn operation of the Hejaz Railway in spite of T.E. Lawrence's best endeavours. Russia, invariably short of railways where it really needed them most, took the concept of the armoured train to something approaching its ultimate development. Britain, meanwhile, at the last gasp managed to impose order on the potential chaos of its fragmented railways and in time relearned the importance of railways on foreign fields, making a decisive difference in 1918 when its armies broke the German lines.

The common factor in all this was that railways allowed the sophisticated weapons systems of the armies and air forces to be deployed and supplied quickly enough for them to be effective. The common problem, particularly on the Western Front, was that, because the rail networks were so extensive on either side of the front lines, for both sides winning a decisive advantage in attack was a horrifically costly exercise in lives and munitions. And, of course, with armies so dependent upon railways for their supply, the speed of an advance was ultimately dictated by the ability to extend supply lines in support of their forces.

If the nations of 1914 had had to rely on today's rail network the Great War would have played out very differently. Leaving aside the need to source diesel fuel (which may well have seen the Middle East play a much more pivotal role), Germany would still have been able to get troops to its borders but would have then faced innumerable problems in using railways beyond them. Different voltage systems for elecric trains and different signalling and safety systems (all operating electronically and demanding complex onboard equipment) would require huge fleets of compatible locomotives at vast cost to cross borders easily. This is a major problem in Europe today, and one which hinders the growth of cross-border passenger and freight services. Neither then nor now could any of the combatants afford to make their trains fully compatible with those in other countries.

It is a universal truth that the rail networks in Western Europe have suffered hugely since the 1950s with the closure of routes and stations. Only Russia and Poland have substantially better rail networks in terms of capacity than they did in 1914, but at least Germany, Austria, and to a lesser extent France and Belgium have systems which could theoretically take the strain if called upon to do so. This is not the case in Britain where route closures from the 1960s to the early 1980s stripped Britain of the railways to operate much more than a passenger service. Towns with substantial populations that once had a railway are now many miles from their nearest railhead, and even where there are railways there are few if any goods facilities to load freight trains.

Worse still, there is barely enough rolling stock to cope with existing passenger numbers: in a crisis, Britain's railways would be unlikely to handle today the demands made of them in the way they did in 1914. We have quite simply cut back too far. We are too dependent on road transport. Given that during the First World War there were real concerns that the domestic use of petrol would have to be rationed, the effects of such a move now would be severe indeed. The only real positives for Britain today are the Channel Tunnel, which, if troops and supplies could be got to it, might have been a real game changer, and the long overdue electrification programme of the country's key main lines.

You could say that, with all the improvements in road transport and the development of airlift capa-bility, railways would be irrelevant today. They are certainly less relevant than they were a century ago, but their ability to move large numbers of men and huge volumes of equipment efficiently and quickly is still unmatched by any of the alternatives. They are vulnerable to interdiction, as are road convoys, and their flexibility is limited, but there is no doubt that where they exist they can play a vital role in a crisis, whether humanitarian or military.

When I began writing *Trains to the Trenches* I thought that, as I travelled around Britain and parts of Europe by rail, I would get a real sense of the hopes and fears, efforts and hardships incurred by the railways and the people who worked on and around the trains simply in the act of making journeys such as Berlin to Brussels. The accounts in the book and, I hope, the wider narrative, bring that to life, but it was almost a relief that, when I travelled by train from Berlin to Brussels, from Brussels through northern France, and across the United Kingdom, there were no ghosts.

We are a hundred years on from the terrible events of 1914, and even the greatest leap of imagination cannot transport you from the air-conditioned comfort of a Deutsche Bahn ICE, or an SNCF TGV, or a British High Speed Train to the carriages and wagons the soldiers travelled in to and from the front. Everything is simply too different – the trains, many of the stations, the scenery itself. Certainly Berlin's recently opened Hauptbahnhof is a spectacular station, undoubtedly one of the finest in Europe. Equally, and by contrast, the Highland Main Line from Perth to Inverness and Thurso remains as pretty as it was in John Meikle's day; but even if you travel on the routes, the prospect of being sent to fight a global war is beyond the experience or imagination of almost anyone who wasn't involved in the Second World War, never mind the First.

This is something to be celebrated. That we can cross borders so easily and be among friends is a crowning and under-appreciated achievement on the part of the formerly warring countries of Europe. That generations of people in Britain, France, Belgium, Germany, Austria, Hungary, Turkey and many other countries haven't faced the horror of mass mobilisation, of trench warfare and the prospect of serious injury and death should be regarded as a privilege. We rightly remember the combatants of the Great War, but the railwaymen of all sides deserve commemoration, too. Under difficult conditions and often under fire, they did their bit for their countries and they often did it with breath-taking bravery and brilliance.

Right: The coffin bearing the 'Unknown Warrior' loaded on to a train in northern France for its final journey via the English Channel to its final resting place in Westminster Abbey in 1920.

THOMAS COOK MAPS

RAILWAY MAP OF NORTHERN FRANCE

By 1914 the British travel company Thomas Cook had established an enviable reputation for its European railway timetables and maps. The first recognised travel company in the world, it provided independent travellers with the information they needed to see Europe, parts of Africa and the Middle East by rail. The following maps illustrate the extent of the railway networks of the main combatants.

They may have 'only' been tourist maps, but for British officers landing in 1914 they were often the only guides available until Military Intelligence had caught up with the demand for detailed military maps.

The most useful of all was this map of northern France which also includes Belgium, Luxembourg, the Netherlands and parts of Germany that would become household names over the next four years.

Most importantly of all, these were scale maps and they provided an at-a-glance indication of where a unit was and where it needed to go.

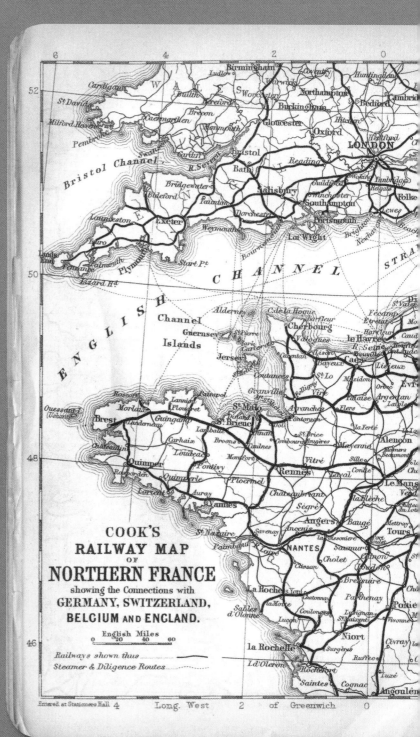

THOMAS COOK MAPS

RAILWAY MAP OF NORTHERN GERMANY

Even though not all railways are included, the extent of Germany's public network which passengers can travel on is impressive. Few major centres were far from a railway line, and the service pattern meant that it was possible to travel relatively easily between any two points.

In Russia, however, the rail network was much less concentrated. The military consequences of this were that unless they happened to be near a railway line the soldiers and horses were dependent on an undeveloped road system, and took longer to deploy.

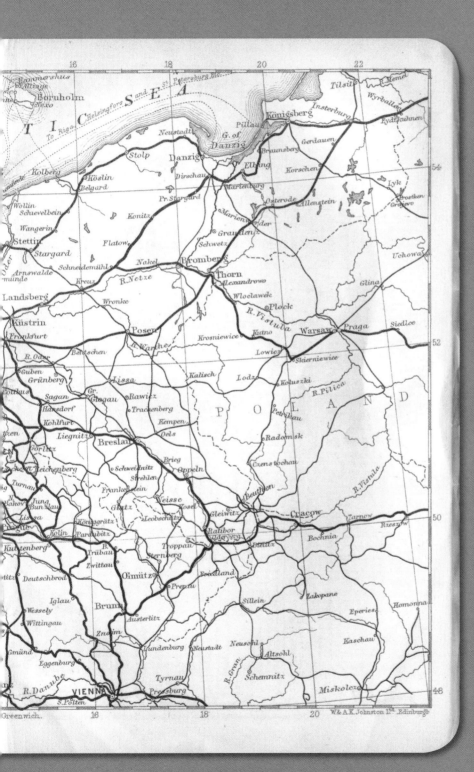

THOMAS COOK MAPS

RAILWAY MAP OF AUSTRIA-HUNGARY

Austria-Hungary's network was centred on Vienna and Budapest, and the principal towns and cities are well served. Unlike Germany, however, Austria didn't build strategic railways to serve potential battle areas, particularly in Galicia. It would pay the price for this when the Russians attacked and its forces were outmanoeuvred.

Behind the Alps the Austrians built an east–west railway which allowed them to move forces laterally; the Italians on the other side of the mountains never had such a route.

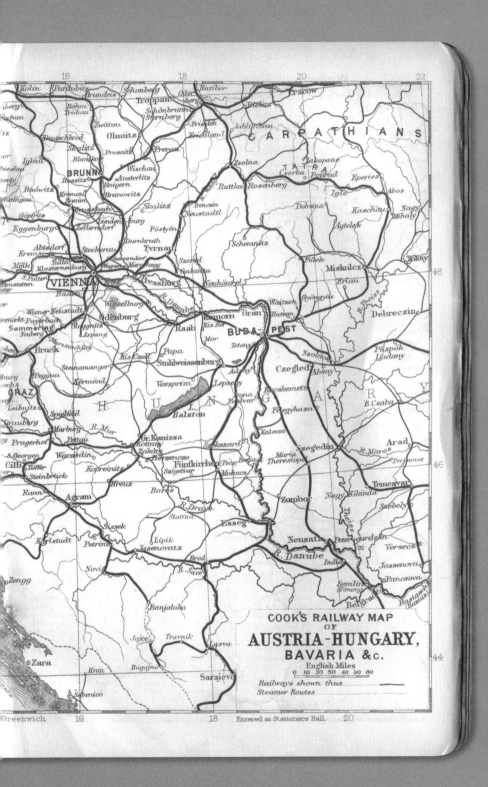

THOMAS COOK MAPS

RAILWAY MAP OF SOUTHERN FRANCE

It wasn't just the railways of northern France that served the country well. A concerted policy of linking communities meant that the whole of France had a rail network of surprising density given the wide spread of population.

Crucially, the two major ports of Marseilles and Toulon were accessible from the rest of the country and many thousands of Allied soldiers, including the considerable and highly regarded Indian Divisions, disembarked at these ports, as well as many French colonial troops from Africa.

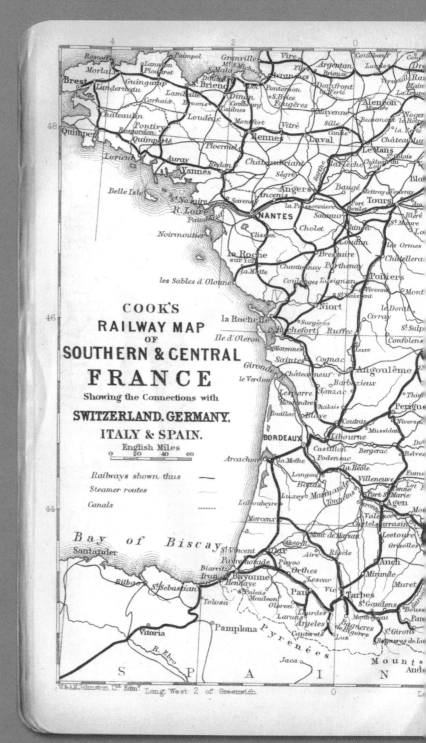

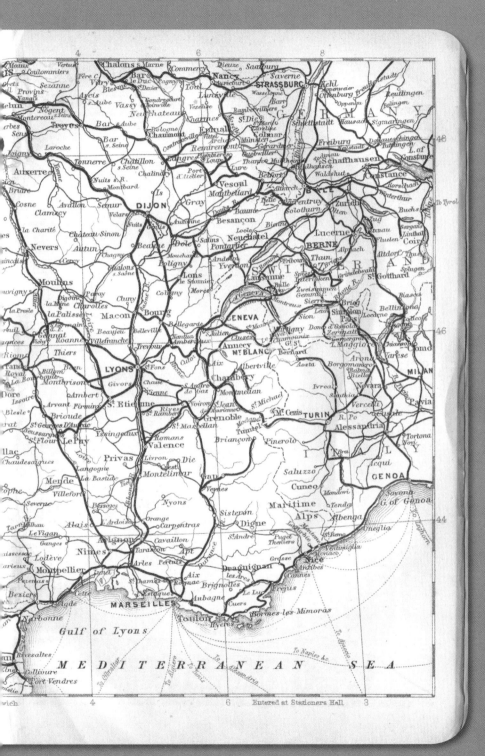

THOMAS COOK MAPS

RAILWAY MAP OF SWITZERLAND

Switzerland was neutral throughout the Great War, and although its railways are well integrated with the rest of Europe's today, in 1914 it was still a work in progress. Without the ability to cross Switzerland, the Alps provided a formidable barrier which hindered military links between France and Italy, with only a coastal railway linking the two.

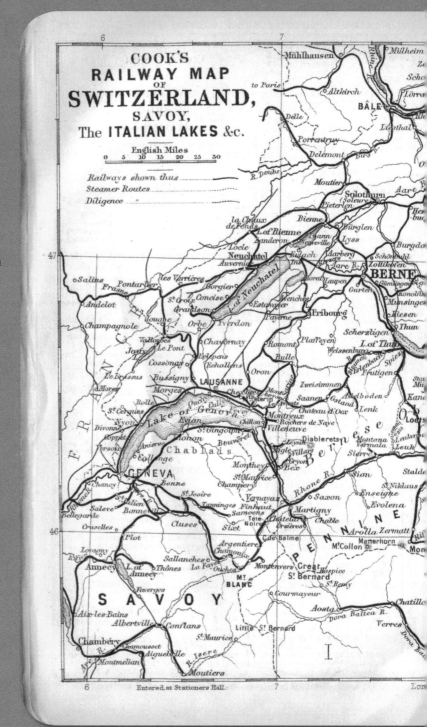

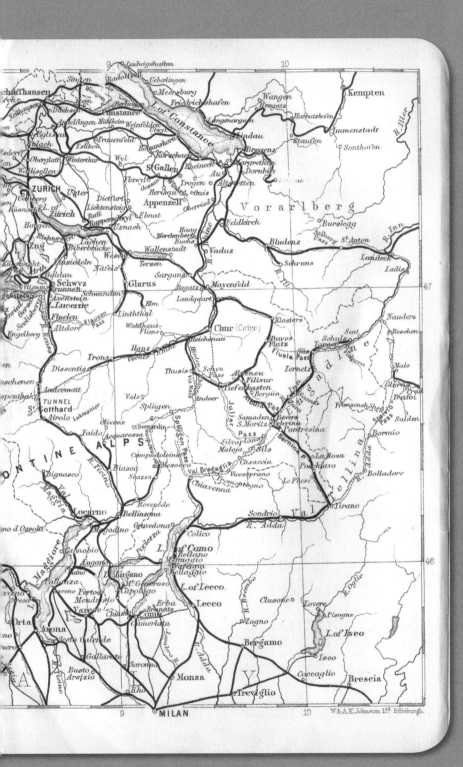

THOMAS COOK MAPS

RAILWAY MAP OF NORTHERN ITALY

Italy's rail network was largely centred on Milan and the industrial north. Links around Milan were excellent and the Simplon and Gotthard Tunnels provided valuable north–south links, but when Italy joined the Allies those links to Germany became unavailable. The only major railway between Italy and France ran from Marseilles to Genoa; thankfully, this was a main line and when Italy needed reinforcements it was absolutely crucial.

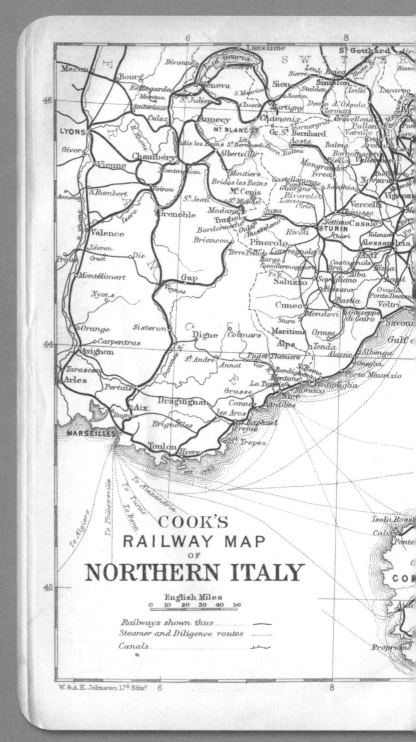

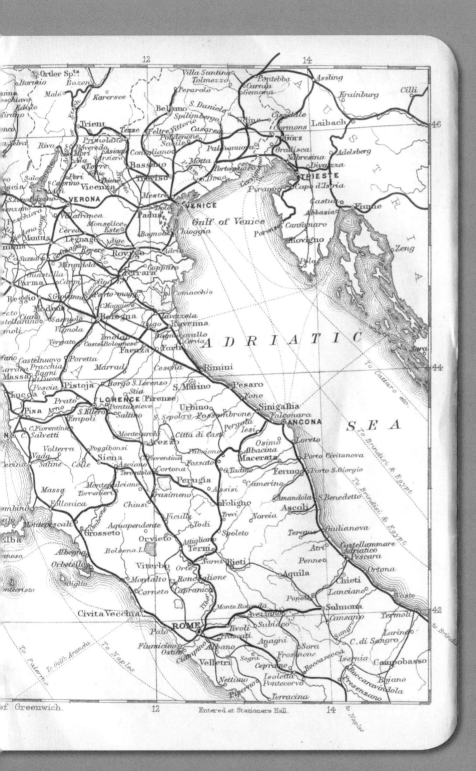

THOMAS COOK MAPS

RAILWAY MAP OF SOUTHERN ITALY

By contrast, Italy's relatively undeveloped south had sparse rail links. Even so, the vital ports of Taranto and Brindisi were well served by north–south rail links, meaning that Italy's growing and highly professional navy could respond to any Austrian threat in the Adriatic.

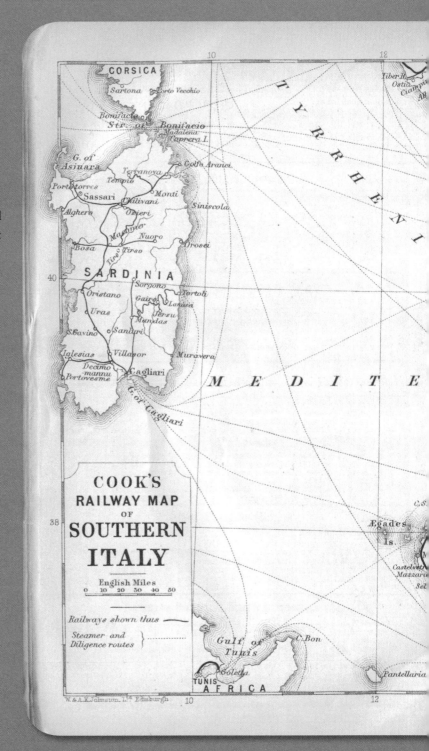

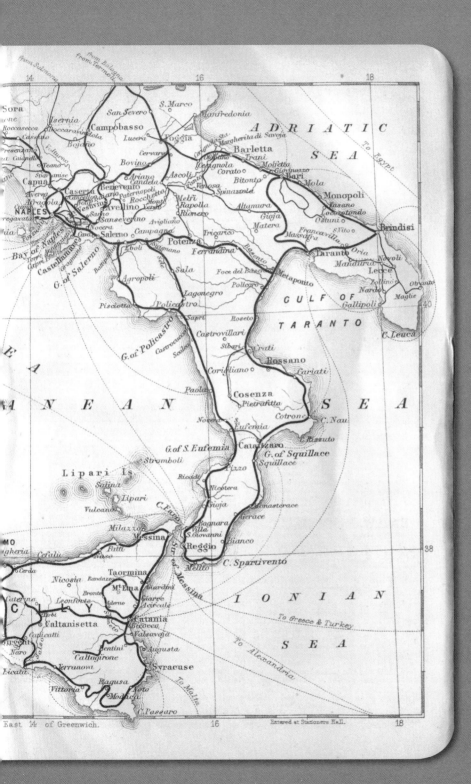

THOMAS COOK MAPS

RAILWAY MAP OF THE MEDITERRANEAN

In 1914 the railways of the Middle East were incomplete – the British route from Cairo to Gaza was built during the war – but the Hejaz Railway from present-day Syria to Medina was in operation from Damascus and serving military and civilian interests alike.

The proposed Berlin–Baghdad railway is shown from Constantinople as far as Mamoure with a dotted line beyond showing the long-term plan for this route. Had it been completed by 1914 the war in the Middle East could have been very different.

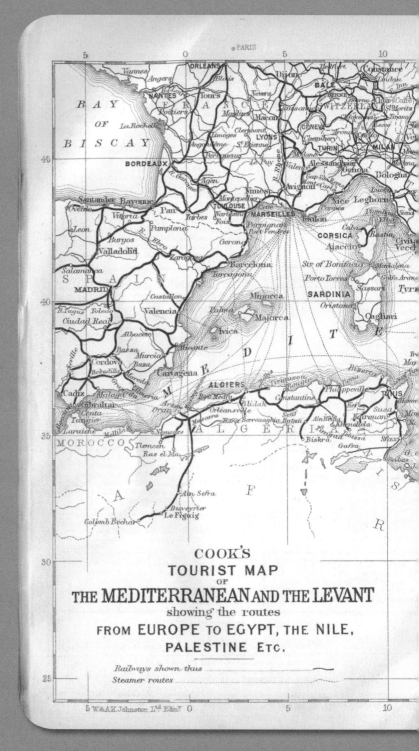

INDEX

ACKNOWLEDGEMENTS

As ever, there is a whole host of people without whom *Trains to the Trenches* simply wouldn't have happened. Firstly, I must thank the railway historian and writer Nick Deacon and his wife Sandie who have assisted diligently, tirelessly and patiently helping me research the railway and military aspects of the book, checked copy for inaccuracies and been the most wonderful sounding boards for so much of the project.

Thanks, too, for Irena Cornwell's help in translating often technical and impenetrable German documents into English and in offering a German perspective on events that the book might otherwise have lacked.

Once again, Bob Gwynne and the Search Engine team at the National Railway Museum in York have been tremendously helpful, offering insight into less than obvious sources of information that I might otherwise have missed. His counterpart at the DB Museum in Nuremburg, Christina Block, opened the doors to the archives there and helped shine a light on Germany's often overlooked railway efforts. The staff at the British Red Cross archives in London were also incredibly helpful, giving us the information we needed to highlight the vitally important part that the ambulance trains and the doctors and nurses who manned them played. John Yellowlees of First ScotRail deserves particular thanks for introducing me to the story of John Meikle, VC, and allowing us to pay tribute to a railwayman who joined the colours, served heroically and is now almost forgotten.

Nigel Bowman of the Launceston Steam Railway has been a fount of knowledge and suggestions from the start of the book, and old friends and colleagues – most notably Richard Clinnick of *RAIL*, Andrew Fowler, Mike Wild of *Hornby Magazine* and timeserved railwayman Tim Naylor have all chipped in with valuable suggestions and opinions.

Finally, I must thank the wonderful team at Aurum Press for their help, support and encouragement in bringing this book to fruition. Publisher Iain MacGregor, editor Lucy Warburton, picture researcher Charlotte Coulthard, publicity manager Liz Somers, and, finally, my copy editor, Richard Collins, who has polished the text, corrected inconsistencies and ensured that the words that reached the pages were as good as they possibly could be.

In a sense, each chapter in this book could easily be expanded into a book in its own right – certainly there is much of interest that could be covered in more detail. If you have any comments on the book please visit my website at www.andrewroden.com

BIBLIOGRAPHY

Selected Bibliography

Aves, William A.T., *R.O.D. The Railway Operating Division on the Western Front: The Royal Engineers in France and Belgium 1915–1919*, Shaun Tyas, 2009.

Corrigan, Gordon, *Mud, Blood and Poppycock*, Cassell, 2003.

Dingwall Museum Trust, *Portrait of a Soldier*, Dingwall Museum Trust, 1992.

Dow, George, *Great Central*, Vol. 3, *Fay Sets the Pace 1900–1922*, Locomotive Publishing Co., 1971.

Faulkner, J.N., and Williams, R.A., *The LSWR In The Twentieth Century*, David & Charles, 1988.

Haig, Douglas, *War Diaries and Letters 1914–1918,* BCA, 2005.

Hamilton, J.A.B., *Britain's Railways in World War 1*, George Allen & Unwin, 1969.

Hammerton, Sir John (ed.), *The Great War. I Was There*, Vols I–3, Amalgamated Press, 1938.

Hastings, Max, *Catastrophe: Europe Goes to War 1914*, William Collins, 2013.

Henniker, Col. A.M., *Transportation on the Western Front 1914–18*, HMSO, 1937.

Holmes, Richard, *The Western Front*, BBC Books, 1999.

Karau, Paul, Parsons, Mike, and Robertson, Kevin, *The Didcot Newbury and Southampton Railway*, Wild Swan Publishing, 1981.

Lawrence, T.E., *Seven Pillars of Wisdom*, Reprint Society Ltd, 1939.

Liddell Hart, B.H., *History of the First World War*, BCA, 1982.

Locomotives of the LNER Part 6B, The Railway Correspondence and Travel Society, 1983.

Macdonald, Lyn, *1914*, Michael Joseph, 1987.

— *The Roses of No-Man's Land*, Macmillan Papermac, 1988.

Maggs, Colin, *The Midland & South Western Junction Railway*, David & Charles, 1967.

Massie, Robert K., *Nicholas and Alexandra*, Gollancz, 1968.

McMeekin, Sean, *The Berlin–Baghdad Express*, Penguin Books, 2011.

Middlebrook, Martin, *The First Day on the Somme*, Allen Lane/Penguin Books, 1983.

— *The Kaiser's Battle*, Allen Lane/Penguin Books, 1978.

Mitchell, Alan, *The Great Train Race – Railways and the Franco-German Rivalry*, Berghahn Books, 2000.

Murray, John, and Neillands, Robin, *The Old Contemptibles: The British Expeditionary Force, 1914*, John Murray, 2004.

Nock, O.S., *The South Eastern & Chatham Railway*, Ian Allan, 1961.

— *North Western*, Ian Allan, 1968.

Norton, Roy, *The Man of Peace*, Oxford Pamphlets, 1914–1915.

Pitt, Barrie (ed.), *History of the First World War*, Vols 1–8, Purnell, 1970.

Pratt, Edwin A., *The Rise of Rail-Power in War and Conquest 1833–1914*, P.S. King & Son, 1916.

Stevenson, David, *1914–1918: The History of the First World War*, Penguin Books, 2005.

Stone, Norman, *The Eastern Front 1914–1917*, Penguin Books, 1998.

Taylor, A.J.P., *How Wars Begin*, BCA, 1979.

Taylorson, Keith, *Narrow Gauge at War*, Vols 1 and 2, Plateway Press, 1987 and 1996.

The Western Front Then and Now, George Newnes, 1938.

Vallance, H.A., *The Highland Railway*, David & Charles, 1969.

Van Emden, Richard, *Britain's Last Tommies*. Pen & Sword, 2005.

Vaughan, Adrian, *Railwaymen, Politics & Money*, John Murray, 1997.

Wilson, H.W., *The Great War. The Standard History of the All-European Conflict*, Vols 1–13, Amalgamated Press, 1914–1919.

Wolmar, Christian, *Engines of War,* Atlantic Books, 2012.

Wrottesley, John, *The Great Northern Railway*, Vol. 3: *Twentieth Century to Grouping*, Batsford, 1981.

Zaloga, Stephen J., *Armoured Trains*, Osprey Publishing, 2008.

PICTURE CREDITS